SPORTS CONNECTION

Integrated
Simulation

Microsoft® Office 2007/2010

Susie H. VanHuss, Ph.D.

Distinguished Professor Emeritus
Moore School of Business
University of South Carolina

Connie M. Forde, Ph.D.

Professor, Department of Instructional Systems
and Workforce Development
Mississippi State University

SOUTH-WESTERN
CENGAGE Learning™

Australia • Brazil • Japan • Korea • Mexico • Singapore • Spain • United Kingdom • United States

SOUTH-WESTERN
CENGAGE Learning™

Sports Connection, Fourth Edition
Susie H. VanHuss, Connie M. Forde

Vice President of Editorial, Business:
    Jack W. Calhoun

Vice President/Editor-in-Chief: Karen Schmohe

Sr. Acquisitions Editor: Jane Phelan

Developmental Editor: Lisa Loftus

Editorial Assistant: Conor Allen

Marketing Manager: Laura Stopa

Sr. Content Project Manager: Martha Conway

Media Editor: Lysa Kosins

Sr. Print Buyer: Charlene Taylor

Production Service: Integra

Copyeditor: Mary Todd, Todd Publishing
    Services

Sr. Art Director: Tippy McIntosh

Internal and Cover Designer: Lou Ann Thesing

Cover Image: Alistair Berg/Getty Images,
    Marc Romanelli/Getty Images

Sr. Rights Acquisitions Account Manager,
    Image: Deanna Ettinger

Photo Researcher: Darren Wright

For product information and technology assistance, contact us at
Cengage Learning Customer & Sales Support, 1-800-354-9706

For permission to use material from this text or product,
submit all requests online at **www.cengage.com/permissions**
Further permissions questions can be emailed to
permissionrequest@cengage.com

Microsoft is a registered trademark of Microsoft Corporation in the U.S. and/or other countries.

ISBN-13: 978-0-538-45145-1
ISBN-10: 0-538-45145-9

South-Western Cengage Learning
5191 Natorp Boulevard
Mason, OH 45040
USA

Cengage Learning products are represented in Canada by Nelson Education, Ltd.

For your course and learning solutions, visit www.cengage.com/school
Visit our company website at www.cengage.com

Printed in the United States of America
2 3 4 5 6 7 14 13 12 11

CONTENTS

Contents

OVERVIEW OF PROJECTS AND ESTIMATED COMPLETION TIME

Projects and Jobs		Time/ Hours	Word	Excel	Power Point	Access	Calendar/ Outlook/ E-mail	Publisher	Internet
Project 1: Sports Connection Identity		5.5	x	x		x	x		x
1-1	Establish Brand Identity and Standardize Formats	1.0	x						
1-2	Set Up Contacts	1.0	x			x*	x*		
1-3	Develop Organizational Skills	1.0	x						
1-4	Prepare Letter and Envelope	0.25	x			x*	x*		
1-5	Prepare Staff Memo	0.25	x				x		
1-6	Prepare a Handout Using Report Format	0.5	x						
1-7	Create Calendar	0.25	x				x*		
1-8	Manage Tasks	0.25	x*				x*		
1-9	Research Purchase Options and Make a Recommendation	1.0	x						x
Project 2: Finances		7.0							
2-1	Prepare Budget Worksheet	1.0	x	x			x		
2-2	Analyze Data and Design Charts	1.0		x					x
2-3	Revise Worksheet and Create Charts	1.5	x	x				x*	
2-4	Prepare Fee Schedule	2.0	x*	x				x*	
2-5	Research Speech Topics and Compose Outline	1.5	x						x
Project 3: Community Foundation Relationship		7.5	x	x	x	x	x	x*	x
3-1	Prepare Budget Report	3.5	x	x		x*	x*		
3-2	Develop Alternative Budget Plan	0.5	x						
3-3	Create a Custom Presentation	2.0	x*	x	x	x*		x*	
3-4	Prepare Fax Cover and Update Contacts	0.5	x		x	x*	x*		
3-5	Develop Training Activities	1.0	x		x				x

* indicates that the student may use either one of the software options for the completion of the job marked.

Projects and Jobs		Time/Hours	Word	Excel	Power Point	Access	Calendar/ Outlook/ E-mail	Publisher	Internet
Project 4: Information Management		4.5							
4-1	Create and Use Access Database	1.5				x			
4-2	Prepare Agenda Mailing	1.0	x			x*	x*		
4-3	Update Calendar and Tasks	0.5	x*			x*	x*		
4-4	Recommend Time Management Strategies	1.5	x						x
Project 5: Grand Opening		5.0							
5-1	Create Worksheet with Comments	0.5		x					
5-2	Update Calendar and Contacts List	0.5	x*			x*	x*		x
5-3	Develop Strategy for Effective Meetings	1.0	x						x
5-4	Design Table and Compose Memo	0.5	x						
5-5	Prepare Memo and Compose E-mail	1.0	x	x					
5-6	Develop a Presentation	1.5		x	x				
Project 6: Marketing and Promotion		6.5	x			x	x	x	x
6-1	Design Invitation	0.5	x*					x*	
6-2	Develop Article from Outline	1.0	x*					x*	x
6-3	Research Travel Alternatives	1.0	x						x
6-4	Develop Strategy for Advertising Flyer	0.5	x*					x*	
6-5	Prepare Newsletter	2.5	x*			x*	x*	x*	
6-6	Develop a Teambuilding Training Activity	1.0	x						x
Project 7: Database Management		8.0							
7-1	Prepare Merge Letter and Envelopes	0.5	x			x*	x*		
7-2	Create Database Tables with Relationships	1.0		x		x			
7-3	Create Database Table, Form, and Report	1.5				x			

* indicates that the student may use either one of the software options for the completion of the job marked.

Projects and Jobs		Time/Hours	Word	Excel	Power Point	Access	Calendar/Outlook/E-mail	Publisher	Internet
7-4	Use Database for Decision Making	1.5			x	x			
7-5	Prepare Memo and Labels from Database	0.5	x			x			
7-6	Design Announcement and Prepare Labels	1.5	x*			x		x*	
7-7	Develop Handout and Labels	1.5	x			x			x
Project 8: Program Management		10.0	x	x	x			x	x
8-1	Design Membership Application	1.5	x						
8-2	Prepare Documents for SharePoint Site	1.5	x	x					
8-3	Create Graphics and Presentation	2.0		x	x				
8-4	Prepare Employment Announcement	0.5	x*					x*	
8-5	Develop Interview Guide	1.0	x						x
8-6	Research Topic and Prepare Presentation	2.0	x		x				x
8-7	Prepare Golf Announcement	0.5	x*					x*	
8-8	Enhance Employee Development	1.0	x						x
Project 9: Program Connectivity		6.0	x		x				x
9-1	Visit Social Media Sites and Collect Information	1.5	x						x
9-2	Determine Applicability of Each Site	1.0	x						x
9-3	Create Social Media Plan	1.0	x						x
9-4	Prepare and Deliver Presentation	2.0	x		x				x
9-5	Evaluate Your Team	0.5	x						
Total		60.0	x	x	x	x	x	x	x

* indicates that the student may use either one of the software options for the completion of the job marked.

Overview of Projects and Estimated Completion Time

Projects and Jobs	Creativity/ Innovation	Critical Thinking/ Problem Solving	Communication/ Collaboration	Information Literacy	Media Literacy	ITC Literacy	Flexibility/ Adaptability	Initiative/ Self-direction	Social/ Cross-Cultural Skills	Productivity/ Accountability	Leadership/ Responsibility
Project 1: Sports Connection Identity		X	X	X	X	X			X	X	X
1-1 Establish Brand Identity and Standardize Formats					X	X			X	X	
1-2 Set Up Contacts				X		X				X	X
1-3 Develop Organizational Skills						X				X	
1-4 Prepare Letter and Envelope										X	
1-5 Prepare Staff Memo						X					
1-6 Prepare Handout Using Report Format					X					X	
1-7 Create Calendar						X				X	
1-8 Manage Tasks						X				X	
1-9 Research Purchase Options and Make a Recommendation		X	X	X		X					
Project 2: Finances	X	X	X			X				X	
2-1 Prepare Budget Worksheet			X			X					
2-2 Analyze Data and Design Charts		X	X			X				X	
2-3 Revise Worksheet and Create Charts		X	X			X					
2-4 Prepare Fee Schedule	X	X				X					
2-5 Research Speech Topics and Compose Outline			X	X		X				X	

21st Century Skills

Learning and Innovation Skills · Information, Media, and Technology Skills · Life and Career Skills

Projects and Jobs (21st Century Skills)	Learning and Innovation Skills			Information, Media, and Technology Skills			Life and Career Skills				
	Creativity/ Innovation	Critical Thinking/ Problem Solving	Communication/ Collaboration	Information Literacy	Media Literacy	ITC Literacy	Flexibility/ Adaptability	Initiative/ Self-direction	Social/ Cross-Cultural Skills	Productivity/ Accountability	Leadership/ Responsibility
Project 3: Community Foundation Relationship		X	X			X			X		X
3-1 Prepare Budget Report			X			X					
3-2 Develop Alternative Budget Plan		X									
3-3 Create a Custom Presentation			X			X					
3-4 Prepare Fax Cover and Update Contacts						X					
3-5 Developing Training Activities			X	X		X			X		X
Project 4: Information Management			X	X					X	X	X
4-1 Create and Use Access Database						X					
4-2 Prepare Agenda Mailing			X	X		X					
4-3 Update Calendar and Tasks			X			X				X	
4-4 Recommend Time Management Strategies			X			X				X	
Project 5: Grand Opening											
5-1 Create Worksheet with Comments			X	X		X			X		X
5-2 Update Calendar and Contacts List				X		X					X
5-3 Develop Strategy for Effective Meetings			X	X							X

21st Century Skills

	Projects and Jobs	Creativity/Innovation	Critical Thinking/Problem Solving	Communication/Collaboration	Information Literacy	Media Literacy	ITC Literacy	Flexibility/Adaptability	Initiative/Self-direction	Social/Cross-Cultural Skills	Productivity/Accountability	Leadership/Responsibility
		Learning and Innovation Skills			**Information, Media, and Technology Skills**			**Life and Career Skills**				
5-4	Design Table and Compose Memo			×			×					
5-5	Prepare Memo and Compose E-mail			×			×					
5-6	Develop a Presentation			×	×		×					
	Project 6: Marketing and Promotion		×	×	×	×	×			×		×
6-1	Design Invitation			×			×					
6-2	Develop Article from Outline			×			×					
6-3	Research Travel Alternatives		×		×							
6-4	Develop Strategy for Advertising Flyer			×		×	×					
6-5	Prepare Newsletter			×		×	×					
6-6	Develop a Teambuilding Training Activity									×		×
	Project 7: Database Management	×	×		×		×					
7-1	Prepare Merge Letter and Envelopes						×				×	
7-2	Create Database Tables with Relationships		×				×				×	
7-3	Create Database Table, Form, and Report		×				×				×	
7-4	Use Database for Decision Making		×		×		×					

21st Century Skills — Projects and Jobs	Learning and Innovation Skills			Information, Media, and Technology Skills			Life and Career Skills				
	Creativity/ Innovation	Critical Thinking/ Problem Solving	Communication/ Collaboration	Information Literacy	Media Literacy	ITC Literacy	Flexibility/ Adaptability	Initiative/ Self-direction	Social/ Cross-Cultural Skills	Productivity/ Accountability	Leadership/ Responsibility
Project 9: Program Connectivity	×	×	×	×	×	×	×	×	×	×	×
9-1 Visit Social Media Sites and Collect Information			×	×	×	×		×	×		
9-2 Determine Applicability of Each Site	×	×	×	×	×	×		×	×		
9-3 Create Social Media Plan	×	×					×	×	×		×
9-4 Prepare and Deliver Presentation	×		×	×	×	×				×	×
9-5 Evaluate Your Team		×	×				×	×	×	×	×

WELCOME TO SPORTS CONNECTION

Sports Connection, an integrated simulation, gives you an opportunity to apply the most powerful tools of *Microsoft® Office 2007* or *Microsoft® Office 2010* in a fun, real-world setting. From your experience as assistant director of Sports Connection, you will be able to select a sample of documents, worksheets, presentations, databases, and publications you prepared to create a portfolio to demonstrate to future employers that you understand and have already mastered the key knowledge and skills required of high-performance employees. The four cornerstones are illustrated below.

Productivity

Your documents will incorporate the use of a wide range of productivity tools including cover pages, headers, footers, page numbers, pull quotes, sidebars, SmartArt graphics, templates, expertly designed tables, pictures, drawings, and charts. These documents will be created using multiple software applications. You will customize all of these productivity tools and save them as Quick Parts in the Building Blocks Gallery or as templates for repetitive use. You will automate the calendar and manage contacts and other information effectively.

Corporate Identity and Branding

You will incorporate the Sports Connection logo in many of your documents. You will also develop a custom-designed theme with special colors, fonts, and effects to establish the brand identity for Sports Connection and apply it consistently to all documents you produce.

Integration/Coordination

You will bring multiple applications—*Word*, *Excel*, *PowerPoint*, *Publisher*, *Access*, and *Outlook*—together in documents with the coordinated Sports Connection theme applied in each application.

Communication Impact

You will use the Internet as well as other resources effectively to research credible sources and develop sophisticated documents. You will prepare reports and presentations with effective charts and graphics to produce powerful images that simplify complex concepts. Your documents will be very readable and create a "WOW" impact.

21st Century Skills

You will learn and apply a wide range of workplace skills that are critical for success in your career including the ability to:
- work creatively with others
- apply critical-thinking and decision-making skills
- communicate clearly
- collaborate with others
- access, evaluate, use, and manage information effectively
- use appropriate media
- work independently with limited supervision
- work effectively with diverse teams
- be productive and produce high-quality results
- apply leadership skills

Sports Connection's Mission

Sports Connection, a non-profit organization, was established with a major gift from an anonymous donor. The mission of Sports Connection is to promote good sportsmanship, fitness, good health, and recreational activities for young people in an environment that enhances good community relations. Sports Connection especially seeks to ensure that young women and financially disadvantaged young men and women are an integral part of the activities provided by Sports Connection.

You will learn much more about Sports Connection as you begin your position as assistant director of Sports Connection.

Prerequisites

To complete the jobs required by your position as assistant director of Sports Connection, you must have basic knowledge of the 2007 **or** 2010 versions of the following software applications:

- *Microsoft Word*
- *Microsoft Excel*
- *Microsoft PowerPoint*
- *Microsoft Access*
- *Microsoft Publisher* (or advanced word processing)
- *Microsoft Outlook* (or other e-mail and calendaring software)

Projects

You will work with nine projects—eight of which have been significantly updated to take advantage of the power of *Microsoft Office 2007* and *Microsoft Office 2010*.

The ninth project is completely new, and the entire project is designed to be completed by a team. This project enables you to explore, evaluate, select, and apply social media tools in a business setting. You will prepare a report and a presentation and deliver the presentation to the Advisory Council to demonstrate that using social media tools including networking, microblogging, video sharing, photo sharing, bookmarking, and blogs can be an effective and inexpensive way to promote Sports Connection.

Preparation for Your New Job

The first thing you must do in preparation for your new job is to download the data files from the Sports Connection website (www.cengage.com/keyboarding/vanhuss). You will be directed to open these files to

complete a number of the jobs in each project. Note: Other information may also be posted on the website to assist you in your position. Download the information so that you will be able to take advantage of it.

The next thing you must do is to create a folder to store the solutions to the jobs in Project 1. Name the folder *Project 1*. You will do this as you begin each new project. Name the folders appropriately. You will not be reminded to do this with each project.

Standard Operating Procedures

Most companies establish standard operating procedures that employees are expected to follow without being told to do so. Standard operating procedures are guides that specify the way an organization wants its employees to do their jobs. The procedures usually include a style guide that illustrates the document formats that must be used in all documents prepared.

High-performing employees embrace standard operating procedures because using the guides relieves them from asking how to do things and gives them the opportunity to work independently with very limited supervision.

Your instructor may also add standard operating procedures for your class that you will be expected to follow. If your instructor directs you to use a specific software application for a job, such as *Word* rather than *Publisher* or *Access* rather than *Outlook* for contacts, always follow your instructor's directions. If you are not directed by either your instructor or the job directions to use a specific software application, use your judgment to determine the best application to use to accomplish the desired results.

Refer to the following standard operating procedures frequently and adhere to them carefully.

- Apply the Sports Connection custom theme you create which includes custom colors, fonts, and effects to each document you complete.
- Check the Sports Connection Style Guide contained in the Appendix of this publication for guides to follow in document formatting.

- Use the standard formats that you develop for letters, memos, reports, *PowerPoint* presentations, and other documents consistently. As soon as you develop these formats, and they are approved by the director of Sports Connection, they become the official standard formats.
- Reduce the font size on report titles that extend to a second line so that the title will fit on one line.
- Use the default margins and spacing for all documents.
- Use the Sports Connection letterhead and memo form for all letters and memos. The Sports Connection standard letter format is block format with open punctuation.
- Letters and memos may be transmitted as attachments to e-mail unless your instructor directs you to transmit them in another way. If they are not transmitted as an e-mail attachment, prepare an envelope and attach it to the document. In some cases, you may be directed to prepare an envelope.

- Use the Microsoft Office Proofing tools (Spelling & Grammar and Thesaurus) if necessary to check all documents. Then proofread each document carefully to correct any errors that may not be detected by the tools.
- Pay careful attention to checking numbers—especially in *Excel* worksheets and *Access* databases.

Enjoy Your Experience

One of the keys to a successful career is enjoying what you do. People who enjoy the work they do are very likely to produce high-quality work. The authors have selected the Sports Connection setting and topics because we believe they will give you realistic business experience as well as an experience that will be enjoyable.

Connie M. Forde

Susie H. VanHuss

Sports Connection Identity

SCENARIO

Ms. McKay indicated that the most critical thing you can do as you begin your work as assistant director is to help establish the brand identity and standardize formats for *Sports Connection* jobs. The local media can play a major role in the success of Sports Connection—especially in the public relations area. Therefore, it is important that we use the logo, theme colors, and document formats consistently in all communications. This first project focuses on organizational skills to improve productivity.

1-1 ESTABLISH BRAND IDENTITY AND STANDARDIZE FORMATS

- Create and save a custom theme.
- Design letterhead.
- Prepare a memo form.

Task 1 – Create Theme Colors and Fonts

Sports Connection will establish its brand identity by using its logo and its custom theme in all of its communications in a consistent manner.

1. Create custom theme colors using the following custom RGB colors; save custom colors as *Sports Connection*.

Sports Connection Theme Colors			
Theme Colors	Red	Green	Blue
Text/Background Dark 2	0	80	135
Accent 1	183	65	14
Accent 2	0	80	135
Accent 3	185	175	130
Accent 4	45	150	110
Accent 5	255	205	0
Accent 6	250	220	200
Hyperlink	0	80	135
Followed Hyperlink	183	65	14

2. Create custom theme fonts using Constantia heading and Calibri body fonts; save custom fonts as *Sports Connection*.

3. Apply Aspect effect and save the current theme as *Sports Connection*. Check themes to ensure that *Sports Connection* is listed as a custom theme.

4. Key the following information for future reference.
   a. Key and apply Title style: **Sample Sports Connection Theme.**
   b. Key and apply Heading 1 style: **Theme Colors.**
   c. Key the table shown above and apply a design of your choice using the theme colors.
   d. Key and apply Heading 1 style: **Fonts and Effect.**

5. Compose a brief paragraph indicating the name of the heading and body fonts and the effect that was applied. Save as **1-1 task 1.**

Task 2 – Design Letterhead

You and Ms. McKay discussed the style you would use for new letterhead and agreed on the centered style shown below.

1. Use the Sports Connection **logo** from the data files and the following information to create letterhead.

   Sports Connection   Telephone: 504-555-0139
   5600 St. Charles Avenue   Fax: 504-555-0131
   New Orleans, LA 70115-8264   www.sportsconnection.org

2. Save the letterhead as a Quick Part named *Sports Connection Letterhead*. Set up a new Quick Parts category named *Sports Connection*. Then save the document as a template with the name **sports connection letterhead**.

Quick Parts
Insert/Text/Quick Parts/
Save Selection to Quick
Part Gallery

Sports Connection
5600 St. Charles Avenue   New Orleans, LA 70115-8264
Telephone: 504-555-0139   Fax: 504-555-0131   www.sportsconnection.org

Task 3 – Prepare Memo Form

You need a memo form that can be used for both volunteers and employees. It should include the letterhead plus:

TO: | FROM: | DATE: | SUBJECT:

1. Create a memo form.

2. Save the memo heading as a Quick Part named *Sports Connection Memo* in the Sports Connection category. Save as a template named **sports connection memo**.

Sports Connection
5600 St. Charles Avenue   New Orleans, LA 70115-8264
Telephone: 504-555-0139   Fax: 504-555-0131   www.sportsconnection.org

TO:

FROM:

DATE:

SUBJECT:

1-2 SET UP CONTACTS

- Create *Outlook* folders (or *Access tables*) for contacts.
- Enter contact information for each group.
- Create AutoCorrect entries.

Software: *Outlook* or *Access*

The ability to access accurate contact information quickly and easily enhances productivity. Create *Outlook* folders and enter the information for the next three tasks. If your instructor directs you to use *Access* tables for these tasks, create the tables in a database named **sports connection**.

Task 1 – Set Up General Contacts

1. Under Contacts create a folder named *General Contacts* (or if instructed to use *Access*, create a database named **sports connection**. Create a new table in the database and name it *Contacts*.)

2. Add the following contacts and then print a copy in Small Booklet Style. (If you are working in *Access*, create separate fields for *Title*, *First Name*, *Last Name*, and parts of the address. Add a new field named *Contact Type* and enter **General** for each of the contacts listed below.

Full Name	Mr. James Cleveland	Dr. Barbara Thrasher	Ms. Lydia Garcia	Mr. Javier Ortega
Job Title	Athletics Director	Senior Women's Administrator	Landscape Architect	Architect
Company	Central University	Central University	Simmons Landscape Company	Ortega-Hunter Architects, PA
Business Address	23 Easton Boulevard New Orleans, LA 70115-0023	23 Easton Boulevard New Orleans, LA 70115-0023	PO Box 3893 New Orleans, LA 70115-3893	1433 North Elm Street New Orleans, LA 70115-1433
Business Phone	504-555-0103	504-555-0113	504-555-0176	504-555-0153
Mobile Phone	504-555-0114	504-555-0143	504-555-0158	504-555-0171
Business Fax	504-555-0134	504-555-0134	504-555-0142	504-555-0193
E-mail	jcleveland@central.edu	bthrasher@central.edu	lgarcia@slc.com	jortega@o-hno.com
Web Page Address	www.central.edu/ cleveland	www.central.edu/ thrasher	www.simmonslc.com	www.o-hno.com

Task 2 – Set Up Contacts for CF Directors

1. Create a folder under Contacts named CF Directors for the Community Foundation Board of Directors and place it in the *Contacts* folder. (If you are using *Access* enter **CF Director** for each of the contacts listed below.)

2. Enter the contacts. Spell out street names.

3. Print a copy in Small Booklet Style.

Full Name	Mr. Wallace Brooks	Ms. Lisa Mostella	Ms. Doris Ondracek	Mr. Thomas Fairdixon	Mr. Raymond Woo
Job Title	President	Owner	Partner	Chief Risk Officer	Vice President
Company	Brooks Specialties, Inc.	Crescent City Fashions	Riverview Accountants, PA	Leeside Bank	RXM Engineering
Business Address	PO Box 19039 New Orleans, LA 70115-8329	23 Main Street New Orleans, LA 70115-0023	100 Fourth Street New Orleans, LA 70115-0100	110 Board Avenue New Orleans, LA 70115-0110	631 Pinkerton St. New Orleans, LA 70115-0631
Business Phone	504-555-0193	504-555-0187	504-555-0194	504-555-0189	504-555-0192
Home Phone	504-555-0109	504-555-0197	504-555-0148	504-555-0164	504-555-0100
Mobile Phone	504-555-0155	504-555-0180	504-555-0125	504-555-0162	504-555-0183
Business Fax	504-555-0129	504-555-0101	504-555-0132	504-555-0166	504-555-0122
E-mail	wbrooks@cf.org	lmostella@cf.org	dondracek@cf.org	tfairdixon@cf.org	rwoo@cf.org
Web Address	www.cf.org	www.cf.org	www.cf.org	www.cf.org	www.cf.org

Task 3 – Set Up Contacts for Advisory Council

The Advisory Council will meet monthly to offer relevant advice in the planning of Sports Connection. Set up an Advisory Council contact group. (If you are using *Access*, add these names to the *Contacts* table. Contact Type is **Advisory Council.**) Mr. Wallace Brooks, chair of the Community Foundation Board of Directors, designated Ms. Jill Wikel as an *ex officio* representative to serve on the Advisory Council.

1. Enter the following information for this contact:
   a. Company: Shelton Fitness Company; Title: Marketing Vice President
   b. Business Phone: 504-555-0165; Business Fax: 504-555-0198
   c. Mobile Phone: 504-555-0107
   d. Business Address: PO Box 3833, New Orleans, LA 70155-3833
   e. E-mail: jwikel@sheltonno.com; Web address: www.sheltonno.com.

The Advisory Council serves as the governing board of Sports Connection. A diverse group is needed to ensure that a wide range of perspectives are considered when issues are discussed. McKay asked you to locate six new contacts from the New Orleans area.

2. Select and enter six contacts who match these characteristics:
   a. corporate executive
   b. university professor

   c.   physician with an interest in sports medicine

   d.   sports professional, such as a coach, athletic director, or administrator

   e.   accountant

   f.   one person of your choice

3.   Make sure the group is diverse.

4.   Be creative in locating their contact information.

5.   Print a copy in Small Booklet Style.

quick**check**   **1-2 Task 3**

> How diverse is your group? Did you include diversity by:
> ✓ Age
> ✓ Ethnicity
> ✓ Gender
> ✓ Culture
> ✓ Profession

Task 4 – Create AutoCorrect Entries

AutoCorrect
Office 2007
Office Button/Word
Options/Proofing/
AutoCorrect Options

Office 2010
File/Options/Proofing/
AutoCorrect Options

By taking a few minutes to enter frequently keyed entries, you will save much time in keying and proofreading later. Always take the initiative to find ways to automate tasks and to manage work more efficiently.

1.   Add the following entries to the AutoCorrect option of your *Word* software.

2.   Add other entries as you complete the simulation. Provide a list to your instructor at the end of the simulation.

Replace:	With:
sc	Sports Connection
NO	New Orleans
cfb	Community Foundation Board of Directors
GO	Grand Opening
km	Karen McKay, Director

1-3 DEVELOP ORGANIZATIONAL SKILLS

- Research strategies for developing organizational skills.
- Apply organizational skills to enhance productivity.

1. Read the information below about organizational skills.

2. Using *organizational skills* as the keywords, find three articles that describe organizational skills and how to develop those skills.

3. Based on the articles you read, list five ways to become better organized in your work. Include the title, author, and URL for each of the three articles.

4. Review the two jobs that you have completed in this project and list five things you did which helped you to get organized. Write a sentence or two about how doing these things will make you more productive and effective in your new position as assistant director of Sports Connection.

5. Format your work effectively and save it as **1-3 organizational skills**.

Organizational Skills

Sports Connection, as is true of most small organizations, has a very small staff. Therefore, to accomplish the goals of the organization, staff members must place major emphasis on being productive and accountable for their responsibilities. Good organizational skills are a prerequisite for being productive. Once a project has been planned, the next step is to get organized so that it can be implemented in an effective manner. Part of good organization is determining what needs to be given priority and what can be done to accomplish the job in minimum time. If you organize and automate repetitive tasks effectively once, each time

you have to do the task you can enhance your productivity.

Understanding the relationship among factors such as time management, setting priorities, using initiative, organizing work, and automating tasks enables you to take steps to balance your workload. A few minutes spent in doing simple things such as automating contacts, adding AutoCorrect entries, and using Quick Parts can save you valuable time when you have to meet critical deadlines. Having contact information handy also makes you more independent. You do not have to ask others for information.

1-4 PREPARE LETTER AND ENVELOPE

- Key a business letter and envelope.
- Use the Sports Connection template or Quick Part.
- Locate address in contact information.

Software: *Word* and *Outlook* or *Access*

You met with Ms. McKay to discuss some of your administrative responsibilities. She asked you to assist her in preparing some of the letters and memos she sends to various contacts. You took the following notes about her style preferences for letters and memos:

- In some cases, you will key documents for her. In other cases, you will compose them and send them out under your own name.
- Check your contact information for addresses, e-mail, and telephone or fax numbers.
- Always follow the standard Sports Connection formats. Refer to the Style Guide when you have style questions.
- Use an appropriate salutation, such as *Dear Mr. Brooks*. When addressing employees and close friends, use the first name.
- She prefers the following closing lines for letters: (Hint: Be productive and save the closing lines for her letters and for your letters as Quick Parts.)

  Sincerely

  Karen McKay
  Director

  xx (substitute your initials)

Quick Parts
Insert/Text/Quick Parts/
Save Selection to Quick
Part Gallery

1. Ms. McKay asked you to key a letter to Mr. Wallace Brooks, chair of the Community Foundation Board of Directors, accepting her appointment as director of Sports Connection.

2. Prepare an envelope and attach it to the letter.

3. Send a copy to the Community Foundation Board of Directors. Be sure to add the appropriate special notations. Copies to individual members will be sent electronically.

4. Save the letter as **1-4 brooks**.

August 18, 20—

Dear Mr. Brooks

Contract Acceptance

The recent gift to the city of New Orleans is truly exciting, and I am very pleased to accept your offer to serve as the director of Sports Connection. Having served as director of the New Orleans Park and Recreation Center for the past six years, I am excited about the opportunities now available to our youth and citizens. I am very eager to continue the current outstanding programs, coordinate the renovation project, and direct a team that will bring us to the forefront of sports facilities offering innovative programs for its citizens.

Mr. Brooks, I commend the Community Foundation for the mission of Sports Connection to promote good sportsmanship, fitness, good health, and recreational activities for the youth of New Orleans. This gift will take us the distance in making our mission a reality in New Orleans, and I feel fortunate to be a part of this team.

Two signed originals of my employment contract are enclosed. I have retained the third copy for my records.

My staff has completed all preparations for the 2 p.m. press conference on August 30 to announce the donation and the name change from New Orleans Park and Recreation Center to Sports Connection. You will need to arrive at City Hall at 1:30 p.m.

1-5 PREPARE STAFF MEMO

- Key a memo using either a template or Quick Part.
- Transmit the memo via e-mail or as directed by your instructor.

Software: *Word* and *Outlook* or other e-mail if available

Ms. McKay wishes to inform all current employees of New Orleans Park and Recreation Center of the $5 million donation and the name change of the center. This communication must receive top priority today as the staff is encouraged to attend the 2 p.m. press conference.

Prepare the memo on the next page following these directions:

1. Key **Staff Distribution** List in the **TO** position in the heading.

2. Make corrections indicated on the document.

3. Key **Distribution List:** below your reference initials and list the names of five of your classmates. If necessary, list the names horizontally so that the memo remains a one-page document.

4. Save the file as **1-5 donation memo**.

5. If you have e-mail available, create a group list (distribution list) with the e-mail addresses of the five classmates, attach the memo, and send it to them.

FROM: Karen McKay, Director
DATE: August 19, 20--
SUBJECT: $5 Million Donation to Be Announced

Coming to the city this month as an anonymous gift,

We are pleased to announce to our staff the receipt of a $5 million gift to the New Orleans Park and Recreation Center. The major intent of this generous donation is to:

Sp 1.   Provide an endowment fund of $3 million to the Community Foundation. Specifications allow 5% of the earnings to be distributed to the New Orleans Park and Recreation Center each year (provided earnings are adequate).

and the park area

2.   Provide $2 million to the New Orleans Park and Recreation Center to update and equip an indoor sports facility and to fund the operational budget for the first year.

4
3.   Design sports and fitness programs that will help all youth.

to build good sportsmanship and

5
4.   Plan educational programs that will teach young people to develop a positive attitude toward fitness and health.

3
5.   Establish an advisory council to oversee the financial and operational activities.

The opportunities that this donation offers our center ~~particularly young women~~ and the ~~disadvantaged~~ youth of New Orleans are tremendous. Your commitment to your position is greatly appreciated, and your continued contributions and commitment are very much needed as we all work together this next year to plan Sports Connection. *bold*

That's right--**Sports Connection**--a new name and a new direction for the youth ~~and citizens~~ of New Orleans. You are all invited to attend the official announcement that will be made today at a 2:00 p.m. press conference at City Hall. I look forward to seeing many of you there.

1-6 PREPARE HANDOUT USING REPORT FORMAT

- Prepare a handout using report format and data file.
- Correct errors in data file as well as those you make.

Ms. McKay asked you to prepare a handout for the Executive Committee meeting using the rough draft in the **overview** data file and the following information. She wants the Executive Committee to review the material and make sure it accurately describes the ongoing relationship between Sports Connection and the Community Foundation. When the new Sports Connection website is completed, she plans to post this information so that it will be widely available to the public.

1. Insert the revised mission statement at the appropriate position:

   The mission of Sports Connection is to promote good sportsmanship, fitness, good health, and recreational activities for young people in an environment that enhances good community relations. Sports Connection especially seeks to ensure that young women and financially disadvantaged young men and women are an integral part of the activities provided by Sports Connection.

2. Insert the description of the site:

   The physical facility consists of a park and a converted school that was vacated when schools were consolidated. The vacated school had a gymnasium, a cafeteria, several large classrooms, an office suite, and several large restrooms. The area of the park designed to appeal to very young children has a playground with outdoor equipment and a large open area used for organized activities, such as T-ball, soccer, and other sports. The area of the park designed to appeal to teenagers and young adults is near the recreational facility and has a swimming pool, several tennis courts, and several acres of land used for baseball, soccer, and softball.

Header

Insert/Header & Footer/
Header

Remember to insert a Next
Page break at the end of
the cover page and to
break the link for both the
header and the footer on
the first page of the report
before numbering pages.
Then reset the page num-
ber to 1 on the first page
of the report.

Add Logo to Cover Page

1. Key Sports Connection
   in the Company Name
   placeholder.
2. Position the insertion
   point before the first
   letter and press ENTER;
   then right-click.
3. Click Remove Content
   Control and then insert
   the logo above the
   name.

3. Add the following to the end of the list of criteria:

    • *Educational activities—particularly as they relate to fitness and health—as well as efforts to build good sportsmanship must be an integral part of Sports Connection.*

    • *Efforts must be made to publicize Sports Connection to make the community aware of the resources it provides for youth.*

4. Key **Sports Connection** as the title and **Overview** as the subtitle. Apply Heading 1 style to all headings.

5. Proofread the entire document and correct the errors in the data file as well as any errors you may have made.

6. Prepare a cover page that can be used as a standard cover page for all future reports. Ms. McKay and you selected the Cubicles cover page because you wanted Sports Connection to have a fresh modern appearance that would appeal to your youth population. Key **Sports Connection** in the placeholder at the top of the page and then add the logo above the name. (Hint: Save the cover page as a Quick Part for future use.)

7. Add a Motion (Odd Page) header to number the pages. Key **Sports Connection** as the title in the header.

8. Save the file as **1-6 overview**.

 **quickcheck** **Check the layout of the report.**   1–6

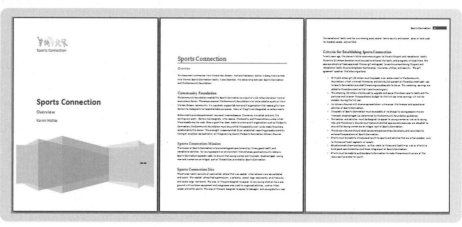

1-7 CREATE CALENDAR

Recurring Appointment
Calendar/
New Appointment/
Options/Recurrence

Attach File
Calendar/Day View/Insert/
Attach File

- Set up an electronic calendar.
- Manage appointment schedule.

Software: *Outlook, Word* calendar template, or a downloadable, free electronic calendar

One of your responsibilities is to maintain Ms. McKay's calendar. Enter, cancel, or reschedule the following business appointments for Ms. McKay:

August 20	Meeting with Stan Williams, Ms. McKay's office, 8:30 a.m. Allow thirty minutes for this appointment.
September 6	Meeting with Javier Ortega, Architect, and C. Rebecca Hunter, Structural Engineer, at Ortega's office (1433 North Elm Street), 10 a.m. Allow two hours.
September 6	Meeting with Community Foundation (CF) Executive Committee, Conference Room, 3 p.m. Allow two hours. Add note: Have coffee and cookies delivered at 2:45.
September 7	Meeting with Joyce Smith every week on this day of the week, Ms. McKay's office, 11 a.m. Allow one hour. Make recurring meeting.
September 8	Meeting with Sports Program Leaders, Conference Room, 1 p.m. Allow one hour. Make recurring meeting on same day every week. Attach the data file **agenda 9-8.**
September 8	Meeting with James Cleveland, Athletics Director; and Barbara Thrasher, Senior Women's Administrator; Central University Athletics Department, in Ms. McKay's office, 9 a.m. Allow two hours.
September 17	Schedule all day for road trip to tour Lubbock Sports Center in Lubbock, Texas. Add note: Wallace Brooks, CF Chair, will accompany. Arrive at hangar at 7 a.m.
August 20	Cancel appointment with Stan Williams.
September 10	Move September 8 appointment with James Cleveland and Barbara Thrasher to this date.
September 1	Meeting with Lydia Garcia, Landscape Architect, in Ms. McKay's office, 2 p.m. Allow two hours.
September 15	Attach the data file **agenda 9-15** to the Sports Program Leaders meeting.

1-8 MANAGE TASKS

* Plan and prioritize tasks.

Software: *Outlook* or other electronic calendar. If your calendar cannot accommodate task lists, prepare the task list using *Word* and attach the file. Complete as directed by your instructor.

Another effective time management and organizational procedure is entering tasks to be completed and prioritizing those tasks. Make the following task entries for Ms. McKay. Save the documents as **1-8 task 1** and **1-8 task 2**. If you use *Word* for the list, design an appropriate format and headings. Save the document as **1-8 task lists**.

Task 1 – Plan Report and Presentation

Prepare Formal Report and Presentation to Community Foundation Board of Directors

The start date is September 1 of the current year and the due date is September 20 of the current year. Make high priority. Mark it 25% complete. Set status as In Progress.

Add the following notes:

> Work with accountant on cost projections.
> Develop new fee schedule.
> Conduct research on innovative activities in sports centers today.
> Develop formal report.
> Develop PowerPoint presentation.

Task 2 – Plan Grand Opening

The start date is January 4 of next year and the due date is February 4 of next year. Make high priority. Mark it 10% complete. Set status as In Progress.

Add the following notes:

> Publicity Pieces
>> Invitation
>> Newspaper article
>> Newsletter
>> Mailings to various databases
>> Program
> Decorations
> Follow up

Attach the data file **planning notes**.

1-9 RESEARCH PURCHASE OPTIONS AND MAKE RECOMMENDATION

- Apply decision-making model to purchasing decision.
- Compose a memo that contains your recommendation.

Read the following material and then complete the activity on the next page.

Make Judgments and Decisions

The ability to think critically helps you make wise decisions that impact your everyday life. In the business world, you are expected to apply critical thinking skills. Likewise, Ms. McKay has that same expectation. She shared with you the decision-making model that she applies or adapts to projects and would like to see you apply or adapt it at Sports Connection.

Decision-Making Model

1. **Identify and frame the decision.** Analyze objectively the situation in which the decision must be made. Collect as much valid information as possible about the situation and what you are trying to accomplish with the decision.

2. **Determine options.** In some cases, options are predetermined. The decision is one of choosing among a specified group of options.

In other cases, you have to be creative and generate as many options as you can.

3. **Analyze options and select the best one.** Evaluating the options may require more information. Each option must be analyzed from a wide variety of perspectives that include factors such as the impact it will have on the various groups of Sports Connection members or on the budget.

4. **Implement the option selected.** The way an option is implemented will often determine its success. Evaluate what is necessary for the option to be successful. Ask the typical questions—who, what, when, where, why, and how.

5. **Evaluate the effectiveness of the decision implemented.** Does it produce the desired results? Can it be improved?

1. Ms. McKay has asked you to help her decide whether she should purchase a smartphone or a netbook. She shared with you her reasons for wanting a new mobile device and her preferences for using it. Ms. McKay currently has a cell phone, but she would like to obtain a new mobile device that can handle e-mail, calendars, tasks, and contacts effectively. Occasionally she will need to check things on the Internet as well. She does not use the mobile device for *Word*, *Excel*, or other applications. She typically carries her phone in her briefcase or in a purse. She makes and receives calls in her automobile as well, and she does not want to carry two different mobile devices. She decided she would purchase either a netbook or a smartphone. She indicated that she is familiar with smartphones or PDAs (personal digital assistants), but she did not know very much about netbooks.

2. Ms. McKay has asked you to research both options and recommend the one that would best meet her needs. Use the Internet as well as local resources to collect information from credible sources about both types of devices.

3. Analyze the information you have collected about each option carefully. Select the option that best meets Ms. McKay's needs.

4. Although Ms. McKay did not ask for help in implementing her decision, you have decided to collect information about brands and costs of the device you will recommend to help her implement her decision.

5. Compose a memo to Ms. McKay that summarizes the advantages and disadvantages of both netbooks and smartphones. Think about the way Ms. McKay wants to use the device as you consider each option. Then recommend the device that best meets her needs. Provide the rationale for making that recommendation. Also present the analysis and cost information on two or three brands that you think she should consider and offer that information as part of your recommendation.

6. Save the document as **1-9 purchasing recommendation**.

For additional resources go to
www.cengage.com/keyboarding/vanhuss

SCENARIO

Ms. McKay indicated that managing the financial documents of Sports Connection is a very important aspect of the assistant director's position. This second project focuses on creating a useful and attractive first-year budget, charts, and the fee schedule for Sports Connection. The custom theme created in Project 1 will be used to format the worksheets, charts, a report, and a slide presentation to the Community Foundation Board of Directors.

2-1 **Prepare Budget Worksheet**

2-2 **Analyze Data and Design Charts**

2-3 **Revise Worksheet and Create Charts**

2-4 **Prepare Fee Schedule**

2-5 **Research Speech Topics and Compose Outline**

2-1 PREPARE BUDGET WORKSHEET

- Create *Excel* worksheet.
- Compose a memo using template or Quick Part.
- Transmit memo via e-mail (or as directed by your instructor).

Software: *Word, Excel,* and *Outlook* or other e-mail if available

Task 1 – Create Budget Worksheet

Ms. McKay has asked you to prepare the first-year budget for Sports Connection shown on pages 21 and 22 using the guidelines below:

1. Apply the custom theme created in Project 1.

2. Indent the subcategories and subtotals as shown.

3. Insert a formula where indicated to compute the subtotals of each category and the total budget.

4. Insert a bottom border to show addition under each category.

5. Decrease the row height above each secondary heading to 7.50.

6. Apply styles as follows:
   a. Main heading of worksheet: Title
   b. Secondary heading: Heading 2
   c. Budget categories including Total Budget: Accent 1
   d. Subcategories: 20% – Accent 1
   e. Subtotals: 40% – Accent 1
   f. Total: 20% – Accent 2 and Total style on total budget number (cell C59)
   g. Numbers: Comma [0]
   h. First number and Total Budget number: Currency [0]

7. Center the page horizontally and vertically and fit to one page.

8. Name the sheet *Budget*. Save the workbook as **2-1 budget**.

Styles
Home/Styles/Cell Styles

Center Page
Page Layout/Page Setup/
Margins/
Custom Margins

	A	B	C
1	**Sports Connection Budget**		
2	Fiscal Year 7/1/20-- through 6/30/20--		
3			
4	**Building Renovations**		
5	Painting, repairs, interior construction work	$250,000	
6	Reconfigure to have 2 basketball courts, 1 volleyball court	150,000	
7	Convert 2 classrooms to aerobic center	25,000	
8	Convert 2 classrooms and 2 restrooms to locker rooms	150,000	
9	Convert 1 classroom to a seminar/conference room	25,000	
10	Convert section of cafeteria to stuff lounge and user lounge	50,000	
11	Improve handicap access	50,000	
12	Reconfigure office area	10,000	
13	Convert remaining cafeteria section to fitness center	50,000	
14	Reserve for contingencies	40,000	
15	Subtotal		Formula
16			
17	**General Park Upgrade**		
18	Add walking, jogging, and bike trails	30,000	
19	Upgrade playground area	20,000	
20	Improve lighting and landscaping	50,000	
21	Add picnic and shelter areas	50,000	
22	Subtotal		Formula
23			
24	**Playing Field Area Upgrade**		
25	Improve lighting	75,000	
26	Add bleacher sections	25,000	
27	Improve drainage and hydro-seed to improve turf	50,000	
28	Add fencing behind batting area and in needed areas	50,000	
29	Lay out soccer, baseball, and softball fields	50,000	
30	Subtotal		Formula
31			
32	**Swimming Pool and Tennis Court Upgrades**		
33	Resurface tennis courts	75,000	
34	Repair fence and upgrade area surrounding tennis courts	25,000	
35	Improve lighting	25,000	
36	Resurface pool deck	25,000	
37	Repair fence and upgrade area surrounding pool	25,000	
38	Subtotal		Formula
39			

Cont. on page 22

Cont. from page 21

	A	B	C
40	**Driving Range and Practice Putting Green Construction**		
41	Driving Range	40,000	
42	Practice putting green	45,000	
43	Subtotal		Formula
44			
45	**Equipment and Furniture**		
46	Fitness equipment	100,000	
47	Sports equipment	75,000	
48	Office furniture and equipment	35,000	
49	Seminar room furniture and equipment	15,000	
50	Furniture for staff/volunteer and user lounges	25,000	
51	Subtotal		Formula
52			
53	Architect and Professional Fees		50,000
54			
55	Operation Budget for First Year (= to 5% of endowment)		150,000
56			
57	Reserve for Contingencies		50,000
58			
59	**Total Budget**		Formula

Task 2 – Compose Memo

Compose a memo to Ms. McKay requesting that she review the budget. Ask her to use Track Changes to make any needed changes directly in the electronic file and to use the Comments command to insert her comments. Remember to use the *sports connection memo* template or *Sports Connection Memo* Quick Part that you created in Project 1. Attach the *Excel* workbook to the memo. Save the file as **2-1 memo**. Transmit the memo via e-mail or as instructed.

2-2 ANALYZE DATA AND DESIGN CHARTS

- Analyze and evaluate data to solve problems.
- Communicate decision using sound judgment.

Software: *Excel* and Internet

The *Excel* workbook contains three sheets of data. Create an appropriate chart for each sheet. Access the **analysis** data file to complete this job.

1. Review the data on each sheet to frame the decision.

2. Conduct research and determine which type of chart is appropriate for the data given on each sheet.

3. Develop alternative charts for each worksheet. Analyze each one carefully and select the best chart for each worksheet.

4. Implement the selected alternative by creating an appropriate chart for each sheet. There is no need to format. The design is all that is needed.

5. Evaluate each chart to determine if the decision was effective. Below each chart, write a one-sentence justification. Save as **2-2 chart analysis**.

tips

Insert Chart
Insert/Charts/click desired chart type

Accountability

Accountability is a current buzzword in all parts of society—education, politics, the workplace, and home. Teachers are accountable for passing test scores. Politicians are held accountable to campaign promises. Companies are accountable to shareholders. Children are accountable to parents for completing chores and meeting curfews. Successful employees in the 21st century must accept responsibility and be accountable for their results. It is easy to pass the blame to someone else if results are not achieved. Think about the flip side. Would an employee be as eager to allow someone else to accept the recognition when results are achieved? Being accountable goes both ways.

Consider these recommendations for completing future projects. Approach each task as important. Do not overlook the details because the task seems trivial. Complete each task, putting forth your best effort. Complete the research and background work needed to complete the task correctly. When you submit the assignment, take pride in the work you have done and be ready and willing to accept feedback with an open mind. Learn from each task and apply to the next one. When your boss asks, "Who prepared these charts?" proudly step forward and say, "I did." Then, be prepared with confidence to justify your decisions and to accept any consequences.

2-3   REVISE WORKSHEET AND CREATE CHARTS

- *Revise Excel* worksheet.
- Create bar chart.
- Create pie chart.
- Compose a memo using the template or Quick Part.
- Transmit memo via e-mail (or as directed by your instructor).

Software: *Excel* and *Word* or *Outlook* or other e-mail if available

Task 1 – Revise Budget Worksheet

Ms. McKay has returned her revisions to the budget worksheet you created earlier. Open the data file **budget revisions** and make the two requested changes to add a custom footer and to add Grand Opening as a new budget category. The new budget total should be $2,000,000. Delete the comments. Save as **2-3 revised budget**.

Task 2 – Create Bar Chart

Ms. McKay needs an attractive bar chart that compares the ten budget categories and has requested you to prepare a draft for her review. Follow the steps below to create a bar chart on a new sheet:

1. Select and copy the ten cells that hold the names of the budget categories. Paste on *Sheet2* beginning at A1. Edit the lengthy category titles as shown on page 25.

2. In B1 create a link to the budgeted amount for the first category, Building Renovation. Key =. Click the *Budget* sheet tab and click C15 that displays the total for the Building Renovation category. Press ENTER. Repeat for the other categories. (Note: If changes are made to the budget, the bar chart will be updated automatically.)

3. Create a clustered bar chart and format as follows:
   a. Apply Layout 1 and Style 10.
   b. Display values on the horizontal (value) axis in thousands.
   c. Format the chart area with Light Orange – Accent 6.
   d. Key a chart title and format attractively.
   e. Insert a text box and key the note related to the endowment. Be sure to key the * next to Endowment in the worksheet so it appears on the chart.
   f. Insert a shape as shown to display the total budget.

4. Rename the new sheet *Bar Chart*. Position the bar chart as the second sheet. Save as **2-3 bar chart**.

Footer
Insert/Text/Header & Footer/click Go to Footer

Delete Comments
Review/Comments/Delete

Format Axis
Chart Tools Layout/Current Selection/Select desired axis/ Format Selection

Insert Text Box
Chart Tools Layout/ Insert/ Text Box

quickcheck Check your bar chart.

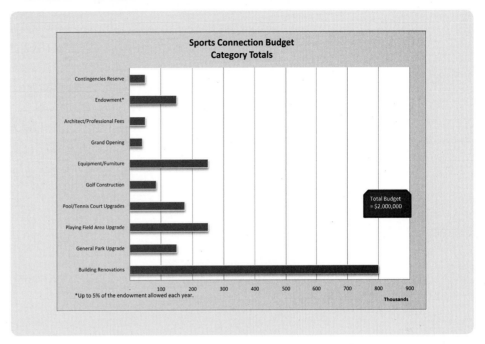

Task 3 – Create Pie Chart

Ms. McKay has also requested a pie chart that shows the projected costs for the grand opening of Sports Connection.

1. From the *Budget* sheet, select the three categories and data for the grand opening category. Create a 3-D pie chart as follows:
    a. Apply Style 10.
    b. Format the chart area with Light Orange – Accent 6.
    c. Key a chart title and format attractively.
    d. Format data labels as Outside End. Show category and percentage.
    e. Insert a shape as shown to display the total budget.

2. Rename the sheet as *Pie Chart.* Position the pie chart after the bar chart. Save as **2-3 pie chart**.

 quickcheck **Check your pie chart.**   **2-3 Task 3**

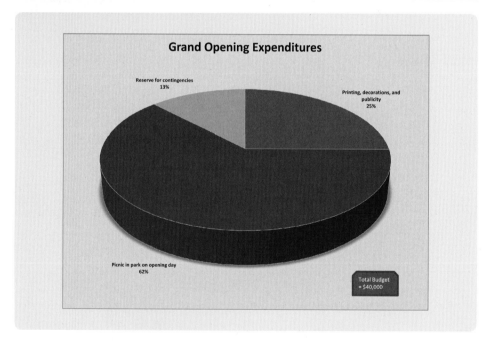

Task 4 – Compose Memo

Compose a memo to Ms. McKay requesting that she review the bar chart and the pie chart. Attach the *Excel* workbook to the memo. Save the file as **2-3 memo**. Transmit the memo via e-mail or as instructed.

2-4 PREPARE FEE SCHEDULE

- Create *Excel* worksheet.
- Answer inquiries using worksheet.
- Design promotional flyer.

Software: *Excel, Word, or Publisher*

Task 1 – Create Fee Schedule Worksheet

Your next task is to create a worksheet that maintains a listing of all Sports Connection passes, special services, and special programming and the current rate for each item. Apply the Sports Connection theme and apply the heading styles as directed in Task 2-1. Use the Accent 1 style for the column headings and the 20% – Accent 1 style for the list of items. Format the numbers as shown below. Save as **2-4 fee schedule**.

	A	B	C	D
1	The Sports Connection			
2	Fee Schedule			
3				
4		Weekly Rate	Monthly Rate	Daily Rate
5	Full Access--No Charge	$ -	$ -	N/A
6	Full Access	25.00	60.00	N/A
7	Fitness Center Only	15.00	40.00	10.00
8	Pool Only	12.00	30.00	5.00
9	Locker Facilities	8.00	20.00	2.00
10	Daycare Hourly Fee	5.00		
11	Daycare After School Program (5)	25.00		
12	Driving Range--Small Bucket of Balls	3.50		
13	Driving Range--Big Bucket of Balls	5.00		
14	Putting Green (per quarter hour)	3.00		
15	Batting Cage (per 25 balls)	2.50		
16	Aerobics Classes--Beginning and Intermediate (3)	15.00		
17	Water Aerobics--Children, Youth, Adults (3)	15.00		
18	Strength Training (2)	15.00		
19	Flexibility Classes for Seniors (3)	15.00		
20	Fitness for Life Classes--Ages 10–12, 13–15, 16–18 (2)	10.00		
21	Sportsmanship 101--Ages 8–10, 11–14, 15–18 (2)	10.00		
22	Swimming--Beginning and Advanced (5)	25.00		
23	Golf Lessons--Beginning and Intermediate (2)	35.00		
24				
25				
26	* Number of meetings per week shown in parentheses.			

Filter
Data/Sort & Filter/Filter

Task 2 – Use Worksheet to Answer Inquiries

A call from a potential customer, Ms. Bartlett, concerning pricing options has just been transferred to your office. To answer the pricing questions quickly while Ms. Bartlett waits for you to find the answer, create the following filter:

Using the fee schedule prepared in Task 1, turn on the Filter command.
Pricing Option 1: Weekly full access, beginning swimming lessons, and strength training class. Insert a subtotal to determine the total weekly price. Save as **2-4 option 1**.
Pricing Option 2: Weekly fitness center only and pool only, beginning swimming lessons, and strength training class. Insert a subtotal for the weekly price. Save as **2-4 option 2**.

For the pricing option you recommend, rename the file adding the word **Recommended**.

Task 3 – Design Promotional Flyer

An attractive flyer containing information about the passes, services, and fees is needed to promote the organization. Refer to the fee schedule for the flyer content. Both *Publisher* and *Word* samples are shown in the Quick Check below. However, you may use the design of your preference. Add the Sports Connection logo if space permits. Save as **2-4 flyer**.

 **quickcheck** *Publisher* and *Word* Flyer Samples.

2-4 Task 3

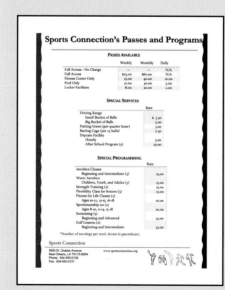

Word Sample

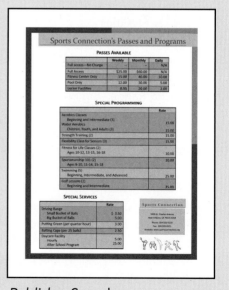
Publisher Sample

2-5   RESEARCH SPEECH TOPICS AND COMPOSE OUTLINE

- Locate information efficiently and effectively.
- Make judgments and decisions to determine appropriate data for speech.

Software: *Word* and Internet

Ms. McKay has been invited to speak for several civic and professional organizations. Her presentation goal is to present basic health information in a way that will persuade her listeners to make healthy life choices and to share this information with others. In her speech, she will discuss how the excellent programming available at Sports Connection is an important part of a healthy lifestyle. To persuade the audience, you must locate scholarly and compelling data to be presented in her speech.

1. Choose one of the speech topics with designated audiences below. Identify keywords and use to search the Internet for articles related to speech topics. Keywords may include but are not limited to *teen nutrition, youth fitness, exercise,* and *youth fitness programs.*

Speech Topic	Organization/Audience
Fitness and Exercise for Life	Chamber of Commerce
Youth Fitness and Exercise	Association of Parents

2. Locate and save or print six articles pertaining to speech topics. Be sure your articles are from credible sources. Refer to the 21st Century Skills feature that follows for guidance in choosing credible sources.

3. Compose an outline for the speech in *Word* using Outline View.

4. Key the documentation of the six references in the Master List using the Insert Citation command. Use APA style and choose the appropriate source type (book, journal, Internet, etc.). Save as **2-5 speech outline**.

tips

Multilevel List
Home/Paragraph/
Multilevel List

Manage Sources
References/Citations &
Bibliography/ Manage
Sources. Key source in
master list.

Information Literacy

Information literacy is recognized as an essential skill for success in the 21st century. What does it mean to be "information literate"? It means the ability to access useful and accurate information in a timely manner. A person must know when information is needed and how to locate information. Once a person has retrieved the information, he or she knows how to evaluate it critically and use it effectively to meet specific needs and solve problems. Today's vast quantity of information sources and the ease with which one can access both reliable and unreliable sources presents many challenges.

Here are some pointers for evaluating an online resource.

1. Who is the publisher of this web page? Is it a reputable organization? The domain name can provide information as to the purpose of the web page. The tilde (˜) in the URL name provides information as well. Generally it means the website is personal and not connected to the domain name. Is the information source objective?

2. When was the web page created? Does it provide current information?

3. Is there an author? What are his/her credentials?

4. Is the content rich in value or is it superficial? Is the content supported with citations or is it opinion?

For additional resources go to
www.cengage.com/keyboarding/vanhuss

Community Foundation Relationship

SCENARIO

This project focuses on relationships—the formal relationship between the Community Foundation and Sports Connection and the informal relationships that Sports Connection must foster. The relationships among employees, volunteers, board members, Advisory Council members, sponsors, members, parents of members, city officials, and the public are all critical to the success of Sports Connection. Ms. McKay emphasized the importance of good working relationships and encouraged all employees to develop these essential workplace skills.

3-1   PREPARE BUDGET REPORT

- Create body of the report.
- Prepare appendix.
- Complete cover page.
- Compose letter of transmittal.
- Generate table of contents.
- Generate table of figures.

Task 1 – Create Body of the Report

SmartArt
Insert/Illustrations/
SmartArt/Hierarchy/
Organization Chart

Caption
References/Captions/
Insert Caption

Ms. McKay has asked you to assist with preparing a formal report. She plans to distribute the report to the Community Foundation Board of Directors. She indicated that she liked the report format and layout that you designed in Project 1 (**1-6 overview**). That format, including the theme, cover page, numbering style, title and heading styles, has become the standard for all Sports Connection reports.

Follow the steps below and on the next page to prepare the report.

1. Copy files **2-3 revised budget**, **2-3 pie chart**, **2-3 bar chart**, and **2-4 fee schedule** from your Project 2 solutions folder to your Project 3 solutions folder. You will use these files in this project.

2. Open the data file **report** and save it as **3-1 budget report**. Apply the standard report format you designed in Project 1. Note that the heading shown in bold in the data file is a first-level heading and those that are not bolded are second-level headings. Do not number pages until you add the preliminary pages. You will insert information at the points indicated in the data file.

3. Use SmartArt to create a standard organization chart with these employees:
   a. Karen McKay   Director
   b. Molly Neely   Receptionist (Position assistant shape to the right)
   c. Alam Khoo   Program and Events Manager
   d. Student's Name   Assistant Director
   e. Heath Bradley   Facilities Manager

   The last three people on the chart report to Karen McKay and serve as the leadership team. Be sure to include your name as Assistant Director.
   f. Size the organization chart to 3.5" high by 6.5" wide and center it.
   g. Add a Figure 1 caption and key **Organization Chart** after the label Figure 1.
   h. Use the Quick Check on the next page to check your organization chart.

Check your organization chart. The chart on the left was prepared using *Word 2007* and the chart on the right was prepared using *Word 2010*.

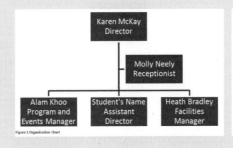

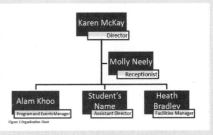

4. For Figure 2 in the report, prepare the Building Renovations budget from the **2-3 revised budget** workbook that you created in Job 2-3 and copied to your solution files.

   a. Copy the Building Renovations section of the budget and paste it where indicated in the data file; click Paste Options and select Paste as Picture. Use Top and Bottom text wrapping and position the object at approximately the horizontal center on the page.

   b. Add **Building Renovations Budget** as the Figure 2 caption.

   Note: Follow the procedures outlined in Step 4 above to present each section of the budget at the position indicated in the data file. Number the figures consecutively and add the title of the budget section. Use this format: Figure # *Budget Section Title* Budget. For example: Figure 3 General Park Upgrade Budget.

5. Key the remainder of the report. Apply the appropriate heading styles and follow the procedures in Step 4 to present the fee schedule information at the position indicated.

6. Note that the fee schedule for Figure 9 contains the information for both the passes and other programs. This figure should be inserted at the end of the Other Programs section, but you may have to position it on the next page of the report. Do not leave the bottom of the page blank. Continue with the Sponsorships section of the report and then position Figure 9 at the end of that section.

Fee Schedule

The cost accountants along with the director of Sports Connection present the following fee schedule for your review. *The fee schedule consists of two parts: (1) Passes and (2) Other programs.*

Passes

Citizens may purchase passes weekly, monthly, or daily passes. Three levels of weekly and monthly passes are available: (1) full access to all Sports Connections facilities and programs; (2) fitness center only; and (3) pool only. Fees can also be paid to reserve a locker for one's private use only. A no-charge full access pass is also available to citizens meeting the criteria established by the grant specifications. Citizens are asked to complete an application from that will be review *ed* by the advisory council. If approved, these individuals will receive a pass at no charge. *Figure 9 outlines the fees for each type of pass.*

Other Programs

Additional revenue is also generated from the assessment of special fees for the driving range, putting green, and batting cage. Figure 9 outlines these programs. Also note that rates are based on *the* number of balls and/or amount of time in *the* area. In addition, to accommodate the number of dual working parents using the fitness facility, Sports Connection offers a daycare facility for parents using the fitness facility. Fees are based on hourly rates *(1)* or *(2)* for an after-school special package that includes fitness programs for the children in daycare.

To fully meet the grant specifications, comprehensive educational programming is required. For this reason, a fee schedule was developed to generate revenue from classes that would require a licensed instructor. Members will be asked to complete surveys, and additional courses will be added according *ly*. Figure 9 provides the fee schedule for these programs. Again, citizens who meet the criteria of the grant may complete a special application to waive fees for these programs.

Insert Figure 9 Fee Schedule here if it fits on the page; if not, insert it after next section.

Cont. on page 35

Cont. from page 34

Sponsorships

their ~~Two major organizations have joined Sports Connection and the Community
Foundation in~~ its efforts to promote fitness, good health, and recreational
activities for young people – Central University Athletics Department and
First Bank.

Insert em dash

Second

~~First~~, the Board of Directors of First Bank has offered to sponsor a Fun Run
on the morning of the grand opening of Sports Connection. Their staff will
design T-shirts for all participants who sign up ~~to run~~ the various races.   *for*
Free monthly passes to Sports Connection will be given to 10 lucky winners.   *sp*
First Bank has indicated a desire to continue the Fun Run each year
and designate the proceeds go to a scholarship fund for youth desiring to
participate ~~on~~ one of the team sports.
in

First

~~Second~~, the athletics director at Central University proposed a partnership
with Sports Connection and the university to promote interest in girls'
soccer, tennis, and volleyball. The plan includes university coaching staff
providing educational programming and team coaching for these three areas.
Sports Connection staff will coordinate the registration and class meetings,
provides the appropriate equipment, schedules playing fields, and sets up
the game/match schedules.

Recommendations

*The director of Sports Connection recommends the approval of the
budget set forth in this report with the accompanying justification.
The oral report is scheduled for October 12, 20–, at 7 p.m. at the
monthly meeting of the Community Foundation Board of Directors.
Questions and/or suggestions will be welcomed at this time.*

Task 2 – Prepare the Appendices

The report has two appendices. Appendix A consists of the revised budget. Appendix B consists of a pie chart illustrating the amount budgeted for the Grand Opening. Use the following guides to prepare the appendices:

1. Use a page break to start each appendix at 1" on a new page.

2. At the top margin, key **Appendix A – Budget** and apply Title style.

3. Select and copy the entire budget from your **2-3 revised budget** file. Paste it as a picture below the title. Apply Text Wrapping, size it to 8.3" high, and center it horizontally.

4. Using the same format as Appendix A, key **Appendix B – Grand Opening Expenditures**. Select and copy the pie chart in your **2-3 pie chart** file and paste it below the title.

5. Add two bookmarks.
    a. Select the caption *Figure 9 Fee Schedule* in the report and add a bookmark named *fee_schedule*.
    b. Select *Budget* in the Appendix A title and add a bookmark named *budget*.

6. Add four hyperlinks.
    a. Select the word *budget* in the paragraph following the organization chart (page 2) and add a hyperlink to the *budget* bookmark.
    b. Select *fee schedule* in that same paragraph and add a hyperlink to the *fee_schedule* bookmark.
    c. Select *sponsorships* in that same paragraph and add a hyperlink to the heading *Sponsorships*.
    d. Select *recommendations* in that same paragraph and add a hyperlink to the heading *Recommendations*.

7. Display the Document Map and use it to navigate to *Reserve for Contingencies*. Check to see that the reserve does not mention the $40,000 reserve for building renovations. If it does not, close the Document Map.

8. Resave your document.

Task 3 – Prepare the Preliminary Pages

Your report will have four preliminary pages positioned in the following order:

1. Cover page—use the standard Sports Connection cover page with the logo (See Project 1, Job 1-6).
    a. The title of the report is **Sports Connection Budget Report** and the subtitle is **Prepared for Community Foundation Board of Directors**.
    b. The subtitle should fit on one line. Shrink the font size of the subtitle until it fits on one line.
    c. **Karen McKay** is the author of this report.

Bookmark
Insert/Links/Bookmark
Remember, bookmark names must begin with a letter. They can contain a number and may use an underscore to separate words, but they cannot have a space.

Hyperlink
Insert/Links/Hyperlink
Remember, you can mark a hyperlink to a bookmark or heading style in the same *Word* document.

Document Map Office 2010
View/Show/Hide/Document Map

Office 2010
View/Show/Navigation Pane

2. Letter of transmittal—use the following information to compose the letter of transmittal for Ms. McKay's signature. The purposes of the letter are (1) to send the report to the appropriate person or organization and (2) to provide important information to the reader(s) that will be helpful in understanding the report.

   a. Use Sports Connection letterhead for the letter. Insert the letterhead Quick Part or the template from Project 1, Job 1-1.

   b. Date the letter October 1, 20–.

   c. Prepare the letter to **Attention Mr. Wallace T. Brooks, Chair.** You have the address in your contacts.

   d. State that the budget report for July 1, 20– to June 30, 20– is attached. Point out that the staff and the accountant for the city of New Orleans assisted Ms. McKay in the development of this budget.

   e. Explain that ten budget categories, totaling the $2 million budget available for Sports Connection, are itemized in the report. Note that all specifications required for the grant are incorporated in the proposed budget.

   f. Refer to the meeting of the Community Foundation on Monday, October 12, at 7 p.m. Ms. McKay will make a presentation to the board of directors.

3. Table of contents—you will generate the table of contents for the third page of your preliminary pages.

   a. Wait until you number pages to generate the table of contents.

   b. When you generate the table of contents, use Automatic Table 2 style. Then select the Table of Contents heading, apply Title style, and tap ENTER.

4. Table of figures—you will generate the table of figures for the fourth page of your preliminary pages.

   a. Key **Table of Figures** at the 2" top margin, apply Title style, and tap ENTER. You will use Formal style for the table.

   b. Wait until you number pages to generate the table of figures.

5. Number pages—remember that the preliminary pages are numbered differently than the body of the report.

   a. Use a section break to separate the four preliminary pages from the body of the report. These pages will be Section 1 and the body will be Section 2.

   b. Before numbering pages, be sure to break the link for **both** the header and the footer between Sections 1 and 2.

   c. Number preliminary pages with lowercase Roman numerals at the bottom center of the page. Apply the Different First Page command so that the cover page is not numbered.

   d. Use the standard Odd Page Motion header to number the pages of the body of the report. Key **Sports Connection Budget** as the title in the header. Apply the Different First Page command so that the first report page is not numbered.

tips

Table of Contents
References/Table of Contents/Table of Contents

Table of Figures
References/Captions/Insert Table of Figures

6.   Preview the pages to ensure that the numbering is formatted correctly.

7.   Generate the Table of Figures.

8.   Generate the Table of Contents.

quickcheck   Check the format of your report using the selected pages shown below.   **3-1 Task 3**

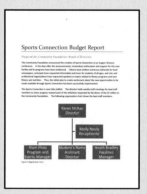

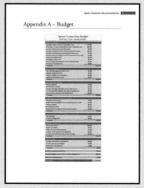

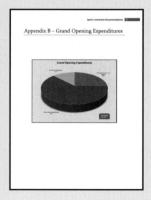

3-2 DEVELOP ALTERNATIVE BUDGET PLAN

- Use systems thinking skills.
- Develop alternative budget plans.

1. Read the information on systems thinking below.

2. Prepare alternative budget plans and save as **3-2 alternative budget plans**.

Systems Thinking

A budget is designed to allocate, or set aside, the funds that an organization is willing to spend on a particular project. Its purpose is to allocate spending in a rational manner to accomplish specific goals or produce outcomes. A budget is used to monitor and control spending. Each component of the budget should be based on sound estimates of what that item should cost. Even with careful planning, overspending in one or more budget items can cause a deficit, or shortage of funds, for the whole budget. Effective planning should include scenarios or "What if" descriptions of potential unexpected events and ways to deal with them.

Before Ms. McKay presents the budget to the board, you will want to help her prepare for "What if" questions they might ask. Identify two budget items (other than the one listed below) that you think might exceed the plan expenditures if something unexpected happened. Think how you would deal with the situation and list the

alternatives. Use the following style to present your information. Use an attractive format and provide more details.

Budget Item: Playing field area upgrade

Scenario and Rationale: When working on the playing field upgrade, the contractor discovers a drainage problem that was not known and will exceed the budget allocation to correct.

Alternate plans:

- Relocate the field to another area that does not have a drainage problem. Study impact of relocation on total budget plan.

- Reallocate funds from another budget item with a surplus or lower priority.

- Plan that portion of the project in stages and complete those stages that fit in the current budget and delay completion of other stages until next year's budget.

3-3 CREATE A CUSTOM PRESENTATION

- Design a custom presentation and save as a template.
- Prepare a presentation with graphics, sound, hyperlinks, action buttons, animations, transitions, and hidden slides.

Software: *Word* or *Publisher*, *PowerPoint*, and *Excel*

Ms. McKay helped you to develop the content for this presentation. The two of you agreed to use Median design with Sports Connection colors, fonts, effects, and with the logo on all slides. Use this design for all presentations.

Task 1 – Customize Presentation and Save as a Template

1. Open a new presentation and apply Median design. Then, customize it with the Sports Connection theme colors, fonts, and effect. Add one new slide.

2. In Slide Master View, insert the Sports Connection logo on the Title slide layout in place of the date placeholder in the lower left corner. Enter Sports Connection in the subtitle placeholder. Then add the logo to the title section of all other slide master layouts. Adjust the size of the title placeholder as needed, and then save as a custom theme named *Sports Connection*.

3. Save the presentation as a template named **sc presentations**. Your instructor may direct you to save this template in your solution files folder.

Task 2 – Prepare Presentation

Use the template from Task 1 to prepare a presentation for Ms. McKay to deliver to the Community Foundation Board of Directors about the budget. Save as **3-3 budget presentation**. Slide content is shown on page 41.

Slide 1: Sports Connection Budget Report
Transition: Select and apply a conservative transition to all slides

Slide 2: Topics
Layout: *Title and Content*

Key bulleted text, select, and convert to a SmartArt Target List.

Slide 3: <u>Budget Overview</u> (Underline indicates a hyperlink)
Layout: *Title and Content*

1. Key bulleted text and convert to a SmartArt Target List.

2. Select the title and insert a hyperlink to the *Excel* file **2-3 revised budget**.

Sports Connection
Budget Report

Presented by
Karen McKay, Director

Slide 1

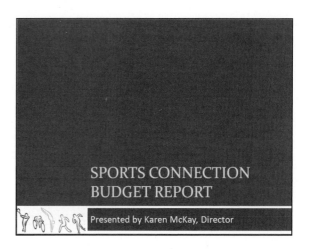

Topics

- Budget
- Fee Schedule
- Sponsorships
- Recommendation

Slide 2

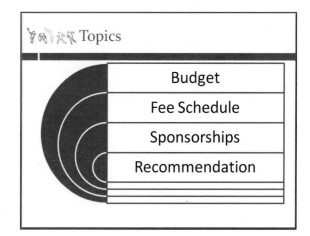

Budget Overview

- Staff and city accountant's input
- Ten budget categories
- Grant specifications addressed

Slide 3

Slide 4: Budget Category Totals
Layout: *Blank Slide*

1. Copy the bar chart in the **2-3 bar chart** workbook (Budget Category Totals) and embed it on slide 4.

2. Check to ensure that the logo is on this slide as well as all other slides.

Slide 5: Budget Categories
Layout: *Two Content*

1. Key the ten budget categories with five bulleted items in each content area.

2. Hide the slide. Ms. McKay does not want to show it unless a board member asks for the list.

Slide 6: Fee Schedule
Layout: *Title Only*

1. Insert a Bevel shape on the left side of the slide and key the text.

2. Copy the shape to the right side of the slide and replace the text. Later you will be directed to add two action buttons to this slide that will take Ms. McKay directly to other slides in the presentation.

Custom Animation: Animate each shape with appropriate animation of your choice.

Slide 7: Sponsorships
Layout: *Title Only*

1. Insert a Bevel shape and key the text. Align at the center of the slide.

2. Copy the shape below the first shape and replace the text.

Custom Animation: Animate each shape with appropriate animation.

Sound: Insert Applause from Clip Art. Play when clicked. Move the icon to the bottom right corner. Ms. McKay will click this icon after the discussion of both sponsors. The audience should join in with applause as well.

Slide 8: Recommendation
Layout: *Two Content*

1. Insert a Clip Art image of a meeting on the left side.

2. Key the text on the right side.

Custom Animation: Animate text by 1st level paragraphs with appropriate animation of your choice.

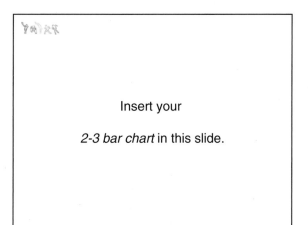

Insert your

2-3 bar chart in this slide.

Slide 4

Budget Categories

- Building renovations
- General park upgrade
- Playing field upgrade
- Swimming pool and tennis court upgrade
- Driving range/practice putting green construction
- Equipment/furniture
- Grand opening
- Architect and professional fees
- Operational budget for first year
- Reserve for contingencies

Slide 5

Fee Schedule

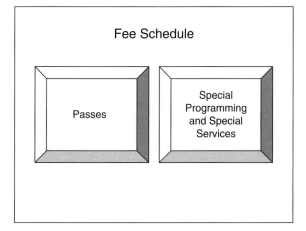

Passes

Special Programming and Special Services

Slide 6

Sponsorships

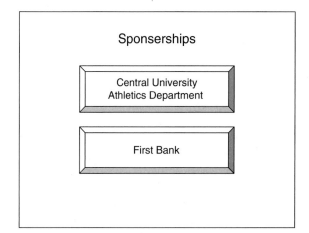

Central University Athletics Department

First Bank

Slide 7

Recommendation

Insert Clip Art of meeting here.

- Approval of budget
  - Improved facilities
  - New facilities
  - New sports events
  - Programming for disadvantaged
  - "Fitness for life" attitude

Slide 8

Slide 9: Discussion

Layout: *Title and Content*

1. Search Microsoft Clip Organizer for a question mark. Try to find an appropriate color.

2. *Optional:* Add a short music clip to this slide. Use good judgment and select the type of music carefully. If you include music, set to play automatically and hide the sound icon when you show the slide.

Slides 10: Passes Available

Layout: *Title and Content*

1. Paste the Passes Available table from the *Word* or *Publisher* flyer you created in Job 2-4. Use Paste Special and then Picture (Enhanced Metafile).

2. Draw a Return action button and position it in the lower right corner.

3. Use the following Action Settings: On mouse click, return to Slide 6 Fee Schedule.

Slide 11: Special Programming

Layout: *Title Only*

1. Paste the Special Programming table from the *Word* or *Publisher* flyer you created in Job 2-4. Use Paste Special and then Picture (Enhanced Metafile).

Slide 12: Special Services

Layout: *Title and Content*

1. Paste the Special Services table from the *Word* or *Publisher* flyer you created in Job 2-4. Use Paste Special and then Picture (Enhanced Metafile).

2. Draw a Return action button to return to Slide 6 Fee Schedule.

Slide 6: Finish

1. Insert action button to Passes.
   a. Draw a Custom blank action button on the lower left side of the slide.
   b. Apply Action Settings to Slide 10 Types of Passes.

2. Insert action button to Special Programming.
   a. Draw a Custom blank action button on the lower right side of the slide.
   b. Apply Action Settings to Slide 11 Special Programming.

Note: Ms. McKay would advance to Slide 12 for Special Services with a mouse click.

Paste Special
Home/Clipboard/Paste Special/ Picture (Enhanced Metafile)

To enlarge *Word* tables saved as a picture, crop the picture and size it larger.

Action Buttons
Insert/Illustrations/Shapes/ Action Buttons

Discussion

Slide 9

Passes Available

Insert *word or Publisher* table from the flyer you prepared in job 2-4.

Slide 10

Special Programming

Insert *word or Publisher* table from the flyer you prepared in job 2-4.

Slide 11

Special Services

Insert *word or Publisher* table from the flyer you prepared in job 2-4.

Slide 12

3-4 PREPARE FAX COVER AND UPDATE CONTACTS

- Design a fax cover sheet.
- Print handouts of slides.
- Update contacts.

Software: *Word, PowerPoint,* and *Outlook* or other e-mail if available

Ms. McKay met Susan Walker, a multimedia consultant, at one of her speaking engagements recently. Ms. Walker was very supportive of Sports Connection and offered to assist with the slide presentation to the Board of Directors. Ms. McKay asked you to fax a handout of the slides to Ms. Walker today (October 1).

Task 1 – Design a Fax Cover Sheet Template

You and Ms. McKay decided that the *Word* template, *Blue Border Design Cover Sheet*, can be downloaded and customized to serve as the Sports Connection standardized fax cover. Key the website name (www.sportsconnection.org) in the e-mail placeholder. Select and delete the logo and company slogan placeholder cells, and insert the Sports Connection logo in their place. Increase the font size to at least 11-point Calibri. Save your document as a template named **3-4 fax cover sheet**. Note: The fax cover sheet is in compatibility mode (*Word* 97-2003). Convert it to the current version of *Word*.

Task 2 – Use the Template to Prepare a Fax Cover

1. Prepare a fax cover from Ms. McKay to Ms. Walker using the contact information on the next page.

2. Compose the message to be included in the comments section.
   a. State that printed handouts of the slides for the presentation to the Community Foundation Board of Directors are attached. Also, indicate that you are sending the *PowerPoint* file as an attachment to an e-mail message.
   b. Thank Ms. Walker for reviewing the slide presentation.
   c. Ask her to please call or fax her comments.
   d. Save as **3-4 walker fax**.

3. Print the *3-3 budget presentation* slide handouts four to a page and use landscape orientation.

4. If your instructor wishes you to do so, send the message to your instructor and attach the *PowerPoint* file.

tips

Word Fax Template

Office 2007
Office Button/New/ Microsoft Office Online/ Faxes/ Blue Border Design

Office 2010
File/New/Office.com Templates/Faxes/Blue Border Design

Be sure to apply the appropriate style set and the Sports Connection theme after converting the template.

Task 3 – Add Walker Information to General Contacts

Contact information

Ms. Susan Walker, Multimedia Consultant
Walker Multimedia Company
PO Box 9699
New Orleans, LA 70115-9699
Business Phone: 504-555-0177
Business Fax: 504-555-0130
E-mail: swalker@ctec.net

 **quickcheck** Check the fax cover sheet.

3-4 Task 3

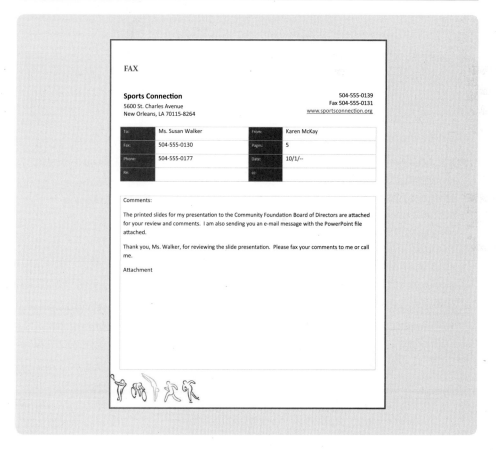

FAX

Sports Connection
5600 St. Charles Avenue
New Orleans, LA 70115-8264

504-555-0139
Fax 504-555-0131
www.sportsconnection.org

To:	Ms. Susan Walker	From:	Karen McKay
Fax:	504-555-0130	Pages:	5
Phone:	504-555-0177	Date:	10/1/--
Re:		cc:	

Comments:

The printed slides for my presentation to the Community Foundation Board of Directors are attached for your review and comments. I am also sending you an e-mail message with the PowerPoint file attached.

Thank you, Ms. Walker, for reviewing the slide presentation. Please fax your comments to me or call me.

Attachment

3-5 DEVELOP TRAINING ACTIVITIES

- Research how to build good workplace relationships.
- Develop an activity for training volunteers.
- Develop *PowerPoint* presentation to use in training.

1. Read the information on building good workplace relationships below.

2. Select one topic from the list and use keywords to search for articles and free activities on ways to build good workplace relationships. Describe an activity and how to use it in training sessions for volunteers. Save as **3-5 relationship skills**.

3. Prepare at least five *PowerPoint* slides on the same topic with helpful points about building good relationships. Save the *PowerPoint* presentation as **3-5 relationship skills**.

Build Good Workplace Relationships

Ms. McKay emphasized to the Sports Connection leadership team that building effective working relationships among all stakeholders is critical to the success of Sports Connection. She asked the leadership team to serve as coaches and mentors to help the staff and volunteers develop the interpersonal skills they need to be effective. A brainstorming session was used to develop the following list of things that are important in building good relationships.

- Being courteous and using good manners
  - Empathy—putting yourself in another person's position and trying to understand his or her feelings and perspectives
  - Sensitivity—being aware of others' feelings and making them feel like a team member
  - Golden rule—treating others as you would like to be treated
  - Avoiding gossip and maintaining confidences

- Building trust
  - Honesty—telling the truth and having integrity
  - Keeping commitments—doing what you say you are going to do
  - Demonstrating competence
  - Establishing credibility

- Resolving workplace conflict
  - Identify the sources of routine conflicts and resolve them.
  - Learn to disagree without being disagreeable.
  - Recognize small things that annoy others and avoid them.

For additional resources go to
www.cengage.com/keyboarding/vanhuss

Information Management

SCENARIO

Key to the success of your office is your commitment to detail and to managing routine tasks quickly and efficiently. In this project, you will create a database, use the database for routine tasks, design an agenda, update the calendar with appointments and tasks, and complete research for a memo report.

Thanks for your great work.

4-1 | CREATE AND USE ACCESS DATABASE

- Create database table.
- Import database table.
- Edit database table.
- Create mailing labels.
- Create and save query.

Software: *Access*

Task 1 – Create Employees Table

Much work is needed if the Sports Connection database is to be fully functional in the time frame required by Ms. McKay. If you used *Access* to create the contacts list in Project 1, open your **sports connection** database. If you are maintaining your contacts list in *Outlook*, create a new *Access* database and name it **sports connection**.

Create an *Access* table named *Employees* using the information below:

1. In Design View, create fields for *Employee ID*, *Last Name*, *First Name*, *Position*, *Wage/Salary*, and *Hours (if wage)*. Set the field lengths as necessary. For the *Wage/Salary* field, use the Lookup Wizard to allow two choices (*Wage*, *Salary*) to display in a combo box.

2. Enter the data for each employee's record. Enter hours in the *Hours (if wage)* field for wage employees only. See page 51 for the data. Add your name as a salaried assistant director (*Employee ID* 1695).

3. Sort the table in ascending order by last name.

Task 2 – Import Sponsors Table from Another Database

tips

Import Access Table
External Data/Import/
Access

Next you want to add the *Sponsors* table to the Sports Connection database. Since it already exists, save time and import the table into your database.

When prompted to browse for a file, locate the **sponsors** data file. Click the option to import; then click OK. Select the *Sponsors* table, click OK, and click Close.

Current Employees

Heath Bradley

0298

Facilities Manager

Salary

Gregory Rickert

9337

Night Security

40 hours per week

Alam Khoo

3816

Program and Events Manager

Salary

Molly Neely

2443

Receptionist

Salary

Chad Kihlken

0038

Recreational Supervisor

25 hours per week

Renea Hinnant

9734

Recreational Supervisor

20 hours per week

Tonya Collum

2039

Recreational Supervisor

15 hours per week

Ryan Sykes

0932

Recreational Supervisor

20 hours per week

Karen McKay

9323

Director

Salary

Task 3 – Edit the Sponsors Table

Make the following changes to the *Sponsors* table you imported in Task 2.

1. Delete records for two companies that are no longer in business: Tours, Inc. and Saints Clothing.

2. Delete the *Type of Business* and *Employees* fields.

3. Add new records for sponsors who have responded with donations as shown below. (Hint: Create a form to make this task easier. Do not save the form.)

4. Make the changes in records as shown on the following page.

5. Sort the *Sponsors* table by the *Contribution* field in descending order. Print in landscape orientation. To ensure that the table will fit on one page, hide the following columns before printing: *Title*, *Position*, City, *State*, *Postal Code*, *Date Contacted*, and *Response*. Unhide the columns after printing.

New records:

1. Mr. Lee Marks, Manager of the Trophy Shop, a retail business with 10 employees, located at 3485 Harmony St., New Orleans, 70115-3857, contacted on 11/14, donated $5,000. Contact numbers: 504-555-0148, FAX 504-555-0144.

2. Ms. Mary Glenn, a partner in Murphy & Glenn, PA, a law firm located at 75 Royal St., New Orleans, 70130-4294, contacted on 11/20, donated $1,000. Contact numbers: 504-555-0147, FAX 504-555-0143.

3. Ms. Jane Bass, Editor of City Guide, a magazine publisher located at 285 Beck St., New Orleans, 70110-4865, contacted on 11/24, donated $6,500. Contact numbers: 504-555-0146, FAX 504-555-0142.

4. Mr. Charles Horn, owner of C. H. Tees, a retail shop located at 1101 Bienville St., New Orleans, 70102-3984, contacted on 11/26, donated $250. Contact numbers: 504-555-0145, FAX 504-555-0141.

Changes in records:

1. Jon Bauer of LA Savings Bank was promoted to Senior V.P.

2. Price's Shoes moved to its new location at 750 St. Charles; all other information remains the same.

3. Grants Oil, Inc. provided another gift of $1,000. Update the record to show the total amount of both gifts.

4. The Sports Locker Co. bought out Good Sports Inc. Enter the combined gift amounts in The Sports Locker Co. record. Ms. Ortiz remains the contact. Delete the Good Sports Inc. record.

Task 4 – Create Mailing Labels for Sponsors

Use the Label Wizard to create reports for mailing labels and file folder labels for all records in the *Sponsors* table.

1. Use *English* for Unit of Measure and Avery USA 5162, 1 1/3" × 4". Use an Arial, 11-point font. Include the fields shown in the illustration below. Sort the mailing labels in ascending order by *Postal Code* order. Name the report *Mailing Labels Sponsors*.

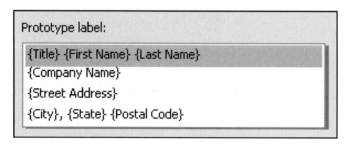

Prototype label:

{Title} {First Name} {Last Name}
{Company Name}
{Street Address}
{City}, {State} {Postal Code}

2. For the file folder labels, use *English* for Unit of Measure and Avery USA Index Maker 3. Include only the *Company Name* field. Change the font size to 8 pt. Sort the file labels in alphabetical order. Name the report *File Labels Sponsors*.

3. Print the mailing labels and the file labels.

Task 5 – Create Query

Create a query to list the sponsors who have contributed $5,000 or more. Include the following fields: *First Name*, *Last Name*, and *Contribution*. Sort the results in ascending order by *Contribution* and print. Save the query as *Contribution Query*.

4-2 PREPARE AGENDA MAILING

- Key agenda in attractive format.
- Print and arrange materials for copying.
- Prepare form letter and mailing labels.

Software: *Word* and *Access* or *Outlook*

Your next assignment is to prepare the agenda and supporting materials to be mailed to the Community Foundation Board of Directors. The meeting will be held on October 12 at 7 p.m. in the Sports Connection Conference Room.

Task 1 – Key Agenda

Follow these steps to prepare the agenda for the Board meeting:

1. Open the agenda template *capsules design*. Save as a *Word* document **4-2 agenda**. Follow these steps to update this document with the Sports Connection theme:
   a. Apply the Sports Connection theme so you will have the color scheme to use.
   b. Change the vertical text box to Brown – Accent 1 and the horizontal text boxes to Dark Blue – Accent 2. Also, change the date, time, and location text color to white.

2. Change the agenda text to Calibri and all other text to Constantia.

3. Set up the agenda as shown below, but replace all the agenda items (except for *Adjournment*) with the headings in the **3-1 budget report** document you created in Job 3-1. (*Reminder:* Save keying and proofreading time by using the Copy and Paste commands.)

Place the Meeting Notes section on a second page. Print the second page of the agenda on the back of the first page for duplex copying for the meeting.

Task 2 – Print and Arrange Copy

Print the revised budget (the **2-3 revised budget** workbook you created in Job 2-3) and fee schedule flyer (the **2-4 flyer** file you created in Job 2-4) and attach them to the agenda for printing.

---

tips

Word Agenda Template
Word 2007
Office Button/New/
Microsoft Office Online/
Agendas/ Agenda
(Capsules design)/
Download

Word 2010
File/New/Office Online
Templates/Agendas

If the stated template
is not available, select
another template.

Change Colors
Drawing Tools Format/
Shape Styles/Shape Fill

Presentation to the Community Foundation Board of Directors

October 12, 20--

7 p.m.

**Sports
Connection
Conference Room**

AGENDA

- ◧ Budget
  - • Building Renovations
  - • General Park Upgrade
  - • Playing Field Area Upgrade
  - • Swimming Pool and Tennis Court Upgrades
  - • Driving Range and Practice Putting Green Construction
  - • Equipment and Furniture
  - • Grand Opening
  - • Architect and Professional Fees
  - • Operational Budget for First Year
  - • Reserve for Contingencies
- ◧ Fee Schedule
  - • Passes
  - • Other programs
- ◧ Sponsorships
- ◧ Recommendations
- ◧ Adjournment

Task 3 – Create Mail Merge Letters

A letter explaining the enclosures and notifying each board member of the upcoming meeting must accompany the agenda.

1. Prepare data source for the mail merge.

   If you created contacts in Access *(Project 1):* Open the **sports connection** database and create a query on the *Contacts* table to extract the CF Board of Directors. Sort by last name in ascending order. Be sure to show all fields needed in the letter address of the form letter. Save the query as *CF Directors Query.*

   If you created your contacts in Outlook *(Project 1):* Go to Step 2 below.

2. Create the mail merge document.

   Date the letter two weeks prior to the board meeting. Be sure to use the Sports Connection letterhead and the Quick Parts created for Ms. McKay's closing lines (Project 1). Select the data source as shown below. Use the outline below to compose the form letter. Save the form letter as **4-2 form letter**. Save the merged letters as **4-2 merged letters**.

   Contacts in Access: Select the *CF Directors Query* created in Step 1 above.

   Contacts in Outlook: Select the *CF Directors* folder in the Contacts Navigation Pane.

   1. Inform the reader of the meeting, date, place, and time. Explain the purpose of the meeting is to review the budget.
   2. Explain the agenda, budget, and fee schedule are enclosed for their review prior to the board meeting. Ask them to send any comments to Ms. McKay three days prior to the meeting.
   3. Thank the board member for serving on the Community Foundation Board of Directors.

Task 4 – Create Mailing Labels for Form Letters

You are almost finished with this job. Prepare mailing labels for the mailing envelopes you will use to mail the letter, agenda, budget, and fee schedule. Use the same mailing label used in 4-1, Task 4. Save as **mailing labels cf directors**.

4-3 UPDATE CALENDAR AND TASKS

- Schedule appointments and print daily calendar.
- Enter tasks with priorities.

Software: *Outlook* or other electronic calendar or if the calendar you use cannot accommodate task lists, prepare the task list using *Word* and attach the file (Complete as directed by your instructor.). Use the same options selected in Project 1.

You consider scheduling appointments and monitoring progress on projects to be very important and carry out these responsibilities with accuracy, completeness, and tact. Ms. McKay has thanked you for the positive public relations you are building through this commitment to your clients and guests.

Task 1 – Enter Appointments

Make the following entries in Ms. McKay's calendar:

October 4 Meeting with Wallace Brooks, CF Director, his office, 11 a.m. Allow one hour for this appointment.

      Lunch meeting with L. N. Skipwith, Mayor, and Wallace Brooks, The Island Restaurant, 12:30 reservation. Allow two hours for this lunch meeting. Add note: Reservation for three made on 9/28 in McKay's name.

October 7 Meeting with Barbara Thrasher, Senior Women's Administrator, Central University Athletic Department, about the new girls' soccer program, Ms. McKay's office, 9 a.m. Allow one hour.

October 8 Meeting with Stan Williams, Ms. McKay's office, 1 p.m. Allow 30 minutes for this appointment.

      Move appointment with Barbara Thrasher on 10/7 at 9 a.m. to today (10/8) at 2 p.m.

Task 2 – Enter and Edit Tasks

1. Make the following changes to Task 1 that you entered in 1-8 (*Formal Report and Presentation to Community Foundation Board of Directors*): Mark it complete.

2. For task 2 (*Plan Grand Opening*), change the percent complete to 50%. In the text area, add Special Entertainment under Program.

3. Add a new task: Article for Sports Connection Website. The start date is October 13 and the due date is October 29. Make this normal priority with the status being In Progress. Percent complete is 25%.

Task 3 – Print Calendar

If using *Outlook*, print the calendar in Daily Style (1 page/day) for October 4 and in Tri-fold Style for each day, October 4-8. Include a footer to show Ms. McKay's name, the page number, and the date printed. If using another calendar, follow your instructor's directions.

4-4   RECOMMEND TIME MANAGEMENT STRATEGIES

- Research time management strategies.
- Recommend five strategies in one specified area.

Software: *Word* and Internet

Ms. McKay discussed the need to implement improved time management strategies. She would like you to locate current research on current time management techniques. Several areas in which she voiced a need for improvement were (1) scheduling appointments, (2) desk organization, (3) e-mail management, and (4) meeting management.

1. Select one of the areas listed above and locate tested strategies for working more effectively.

2. Compose a short memo report explaining at least five tips that would improve Ms. McKay's productivity in this area. Save as **4-4 memo report**.

21st Century Skills

CAREER

Productivity

Often you may hear busy professionals comment, "I had a productive day" or "I must be productive today." Productivity is one of the 21st century skills listed as an essential life and career skill. Each day has 24 hours and each person is given the same 24 hours. Why are some people always struggling to complete assigned tasks, often late in submitting work, appear unorganized and unprepared, often complain of headaches and tiredness, and never have time for their family and friends? On the other hand, how do others appear unrushed, calm, organized, self-confident, on time with assignments that are right on the mark and achieve results, and spend quality time with family and friends?

A common denominator is the wise use of time management principles. These professionals understand the Pareto Principle or the 80/20 rule. They set goals that will achieve results, and priority is assigned to those tasks that will achieve their goals. Their tasks are divided into categories such as (1) urgent and important, (2) important yet not urgent, (3) urgent yet not important, and (4) not important and not urgent. Tasks are assigned a priority according to the established goals. Time and effort are expended accordingly. Applying these strategies, professionals enjoy increased productivity in the priority areas that reap results, increased motivation, reduced stress, and increased time for life, family, and leisure.

For additional resources go to
www.cengage.com/keyboarding/vanhuss

PROJECT 5

Grand Opening

SCENARIO

As assistant director, you have major responsibility for the grand opening of Sports Connection. In Project 5 you prepare the budget for the grand opening, the initial memo to the Grand Opening Committee, and an electronic presentation to be used to orient various groups to the grand opening activities. Updates to the calendar and contacts list are always your responsibility.

5-1 **Create Worksheet with Comments**

5-2 **Update Calendar and Contacts List**

5-3 **Develop Strategy for Effective Meetings**

5-4 **Design Table and Compose Memo**

5-5 **Prepare Memo and Compose E-mail**

5-6 **Develop a Presentation**

5-1 CREATE WORKSHEET WITH COMMENTS

- Create a worksheet from unarranged copy.
- Insert comments.

Software: *Excel*

Task 1 – Create Excel Worksheet

The budget prepared in Project 2 shows expenses budgeted for the grand opening. Ms. McKay has requested a worksheet that shows a more detailed breakdown of these expenses.

1. Open **2-3 revised budget** and rename Sheet2 *Grand Opening Expenses*. Enter the data shown on the following page. In cell A2, insert the date as the sheet subtitle.

2. Key formulas in column C for calculating the subtotals for each budget category and the budget total.

3. Compare the total for the Grand Opening budget on this sheet with the Grand Opening subtotal on the *Budget s*heet. If cuts are necessary, decrease the amount designated for tee shirts.

4. Apply the *Sports Connection* theme and follow the directions in 2-1 for formatting the worksheet to match the Budget worksheet. Set the top margin to 1.5" and center horizontally.

5. Save as **5-1 revised budget**.

Task 2 – Insert Comments

1. Key the following comments in the designated cells.

Insert Comments
Review/Comments/
New Comment

Print Comments
Page Layout/Page Setup
Dialog Box Launcher/
Sheet tab

Cell Contents	Comments
Food	Barbecue sandwiches, chips, potato salad, cole slaw (1/2 donated by local restaurant)
Soft drinks and cups	1/2 donated by local bottling company

2. Select the option to have comments print at the end of the sheet. Save as **5-1 revised budget + comments**.

5-1

Grand Opening Expenses

Printing

    Invitations (3500)
    Newsletter (4000)
    Program (2000)

Mailings

    Paper (1000)
    Postage (1500)

Advertisement

    Newspaper ads (150)
    Tee Shirts with logos (2200)

Decorations

    Banners (375)
    Balloons (75)
    Tablecloths (200)

Picnic

    Food (10000)
    Soft drinks and cups (2000)

Speaker

    Speaker's fee (5000)
    Travel (800)
    Hotel and meals (200)

Entertainment   (7000)

5-2 UPDATE CALENDAR AND CONTACTS LIST

- Schedule appointment as a recurring meeting.
- Update Contacts list.
- Display map and print.

Software: *Word, Outlook* or *Access*, and Internet

Task 1 – Update Calendar

Make the following entry in Ms. McKay's calendar. Print the calendar for October 19 in daily style.

October 19   Business meeting with **Grand Opening Committee, Conference Room**, 10 a.m. Allow 1 1/2 hours. Make this a weekly recurring meeting.

Task 2 – Update Contacts List

Add each of the following three people as a General contact.

Outlook: Add to the *General Contacts* folder. Print the *General Contacts* folder in Card Style.

Access: Add to the *Contacts* table in the **sports connection** database. Key General as the contact type.

Contact information

Mr. L. N. Skipwith, Mayor
New Orleans City Hall
4963 Main Street
New Orleans, LA 70115-0024
Business Phone: (504) 555-0195
Business Fax: (504) 555-0196
E-mail: lskipwith@city.hall

Ms. Marilyn Cade, Chair
Chamber of Commerce
New Orleans City Hall, Room 343
4963 Main Street
New Orleans, LA 70115-0024
Business Phone: (504) 555-0167
Business Fax: (504) 555-0168
E-mail: mcade@city.hall

Mr. Wayne Cobill, University Relations Director
Central University
23 Easton Boulevard
New Orleans, LA 70115-0023
Business Phone: (504) 555-0121
Business Fax: (504) 555-0120
E-mail: wcobill@central.edu

Task 3 – Display Map and Print

Ms. McKay needs directions from Sports Connection to the office of the accountant listed in the Advisory Council contacts list. Use the Internet resource of your choice to locate the address. Print the map and directions to give to Ms. McKay.

5-3 DEVELOP STRATEGY FOR EFFECTIVE MEETINGS

- • Research strategies to keep members focused.
- • Research strategies to involve all members.
- • Prepare a guide for implementing the strategies.

Software: *Word* and Internet

You and Ms. McKay and the leadership team will be attending numerous meetings for the Grand Opening and other events. Ms. McKay asked you to research strategies and prepare a guide for leading meetings effectively.

- • Read the information below on strategies for leading effective meetings.

- • Search the Internet and local resources for articles on conducting effective meetings and especially on keeping people focused on the task.

- • Prepare a guide for implementing the strategies. Save the *Word* document as **5-3 effective meetings**.

Leading Effective Meetings

Meetings generally are very costly and should be scheduled only when a meeting is the best way to accomplish specific objectives. Often information can be transmitted by e-mail, posted on a shared network, or distributed in ways that are less costly.

Keys to an Effective Meeting

1. Prepare an effective agenda.

2. Send it to all participants at least a week prior to the meeting. Explain what is expected from participants. Let them know who should be prepared to lead various topics and things that all participants can do to prepare for the meeting.

3. Start on time and follow the agenda closely during the meeting, keep participants focused, and be aware of the time available for each topic. Think of the agenda as a control system—it should list all topics, the discussion leader of each topic, and, if appropriate, the amount of time that is allocated for each topic.

4. Sum up each topic noting the action that needs to be taken, the person responsible for the task, and the deadline.

5. End on time or a few minutes early.

5-4 DESIGN TABLE AND COMPOSE MEMO

- Apply table style.
- Compose memo.

Software: *Word*

Task 1 – Key Table

Create a Grand Opening Events table using the information shown on the following page. Because you may use this table as a printed flyer, format it attractively using table styles.

1. Apply the *Sports Connection* theme. Set a left tab in the first column at .15" and use it to indent items as marked.

2. Apply the Medium List 2 – Accent 6 table style. Select a Header Row and Banded Rows. Center the table vertically on the page.

3. Save as **5-4 table**.

Task 2 – Compose Memo

Compose a memo to Ms. McKay requesting that she review the table. Ask her to use the Track Changes command to make any needed changes directly in the electronic file and to use the Comments command to insert her comments. Attach the *Word* table to the memo. Save as **5-4 memo**.

tips

Table Styles
Table Tools Design/Table Styles

Table Style Options
Table Tools Design/Table Style Options

 **Check your table using the checklist below.** **5-4 Task 2**

	Yes	No
Did you apply the custom theme?		
Did you apply the Medium List 2 – Accent 6 table style?		
Does your table have banded rows?		
Did you indent the items below each main category?		
Did you center the table vertically?		
Did you set a decimal tab in the Time column so that the times align at the colon?		

Keep the title within the table

Grand Opening Events

Set a left tab to indent

Event	Location	Time
Television Interview Wallace Brooks Mayor Skipwith Karen McKay Recreational supervisor Members (selected)	Main Lobby—Sports Connection	5:00 a.m. (To be aired at 6 a.m., 6 p.m., and 10 p.m.)
Aerobics Special Function Speaker leads class	Aerobics Classroom	8:00 – 9:00 a.m.
Tour of Sports Connection	Begins at Main Lobby	9:00 – 10:45 a.m.
Dignitaries' Reception	Conference Room	9:30 – 10:30 a.m.
Grand Opening Ceremony Ribbon Cutting Speaker	Big Tent on facility grounds	11:00 – 11:45 a.m.

Picnic
    Barbecue
    Entertainment
	Facility grounds	12:00 – 2:00 p.m.

Soccer Tournament	Soccer fields	2:30 – 6:00 p.m.

Adjust Column width so events are on one line.

- Press Tab at the end of each row to separate events.

- Center table vertically

5-5 PREPARE MEMO AND COMPOSE E-MAIL

- Key memo.
- Paste *Word* table.
- Embed *Excel* worksheet.
- Compose e-mail.

Software: *Word* and *Excel*

Task 1 – Key Memo

Prepare the memo drafted by Ms. McKay that calls the first meeting of the Grand Opening Committee, outlines the committee's goals, and includes information to be finalized at the first meeting. This memo will be e-mailed to the members of the Grand Opening Committee.

1. Open the *Sports Connection Memo* Template. Address the memo to **Grand Opening Committee—Distribution Below**. Key the memo on page 69.

2. Copy the table from 5-4 and paste where indicated in the memo. Check the formatting and make necessary adjustments. Use the Remove Space After Paragraph command to adjust space appropriately before and after the table.

3. Below your reference initials, key **Distribution List**. Indent and key the names of the committee members (including Ms. McKay) in alphabetical order. See table on page 70 for listing of members. Remove spacing between each name in the list. See format below:

   Distribution List
       Name
       Name

4. Insert the Blank (Three Columns) header on the second page. Key the following in the three positions:

   Grand Opening Committee
   Page # (click Page Number, Current Position, Plain Number)
   October 8, 20--

   Hint: Be sure to select Different First Page to suppress the header on the first page.

5. Save as **5-5 memo**. Do not close this file.

Grand Opening Committee	
Name	**Organization Representing**
Karen McKay	Chair and Director
Wallace Brooks	Chair, Community Foundation
L. N. Skipwith	Mayor
Your Name	Assistant Director
Marilyn Cade	Chair, Chamber of Commerce
Wayne Cobill	University Relations Director, Central University
Alam Khoo	Recreational Supervisor
Renea Hinnant	Recreational Supervisor
Chad Kihlken	Recreational Supervisor

tips

Embed Excel Object in Word

In *Excel*: Select the worksheet and click Copy.

In *Word*, Home/Clipboard/Paste/ Paste Special/Paste/ Microsoft Office *Excel* Worksheet Object

Double-click the object to activate *Excel* capabilities.

Task 2 – Embed Worksheet

Since members will be reading the memo electronically, Ms. McKay has asked you to embed the grand opening budget (created in 5-1) as the third page of the memo. Embedding the budget as an *Excel* object will allow members to view the object in *Word* with the capabilities of *Excel*. Save as **5-5 memo + budget**.

Task 3 – Compose E-mail

In *Word*, compose an e-mail for Ms. McKay to send to the Grand Opening Committee. Use the memo letterhead. Save as **5-5 e-mail**. Use the following outline to compose the e-mail:

• State the meeting and date, time, and place.

• Explain a memo is attached that provides meeting information and other important information to be discussed at the meeting. Ask members to review the contents of the memo carefully and be prepared to make decisions regarding the details of the Grand Opening.

• Express good will in working with the members of this important committee.

Thank you for agreeing to serve on the Grand Opening Committee of Sports Connection. Our mission is to plan a comprehensive grand opening that will generate awareness of Sports Connection and its programs. We also want to create a desire in individuals to purchase memberships in our facility and for youth to enroll in our varied sports teams. The Grand Opening should help the community to know about our mission to promote good sportsmanship, fitness, good health, and recreational activities. But more importantly, the Grand Opening will spark our citizens and their children and grandchildren to take advantage of these many outstanding programs.

A list of the members of the Grand Opening Committee is shown at the bottom of this page. We are very fortunate to have Mr. Wallace Brooks serve on this committee. Mr. Brooks worked with the development of the grant that funded the improvements and additions to Sports Connection. He presently serves as chair of the Community Foundation that oversees this grant. Also, we appreciate the support of the Chamber of Commerce and the university relations office of Central University. Thank you, Marilyn and Wayne, for the expertise and experience you bring to this committee. Mayor Skipwith or one of his officials will also represent the mayor's office. Lastly, my assistant director and three of the recreational supervisors will bring their knowledge of Sports Connection and the recreational programs to our committee.

The first official meeting of the Grand Opening Committee is scheduled for Tuesday, October 19, at 9 a.m. in the Conference Room of Sports Connection. Based on our phone survey, we have determined Tuesdays at 9 to be a suitable time for this committee to meet each week. Please mark your calendars to meet each Tuesday from 9:00 – 10:30 until the Grand Opening. For your convenience, our staff will provide coffee and a light brunch at each meeting.

During the last few weeks, my assistant and I have compiled grand opening plans of other sports facilities. During this process we have garnered advice from these planners and will benefit from their experience. The following table outlines a list of suggested events from which our committee can begin. Please review this table prior to our first meeting. Bring to the meeting any additions and/or modifications to events and the time table.

(Insert File 5-4 Table.doc here.)

A draft of the Grand Opening budget is shown on the next page. Please review the items to be sure all expenses are listed and that the budgeted amounts are in line with today's costs. Please bring your comments to the meeting so that adjustments to the budget can be made and the budget approved. I appreciate your commitment to this committee and look forward to working with each of you.

5-6   DEVELOP A PRESENTATION

- Create a presentation explaining the Grand Opening plans.
- Add music and animations if appropriate.
- Choose an effective transition to use on all slides.

Software: *Excel* and *PowerPoint*

At its last meeting, the Grand Opening Committee recommended that a *PowerPoint* presentation be developed that explains the plans for the grand opening of Sports Connection. Possible audiences include the Community Foundation Board of Directors, the Chamber of Commerce, hospital administration, Sports Connection staff, city officials, and local sports associations. The content for each slide is shown below.

1. Use the Sports Connection standard presentation design.

2. Apply an effective transition to all slides.

3. Use animations if appropriate or desired.

4. Add music if appropriate or desired.

5. Save as **5-6 grand opening plans**.

Slide 1
Layout: *Title Slide*

Title: Sports Connection
Grand Opening
April 15, 20--

Slide 2
Layout: *Title and Content*

Title: Facility Upgrades

Content:

- Building renovations
- General park upgrade
- Playing fields upgrade
- Swimming pool and tennis courts upgrades
- Driving range/putting green construction
- Equipment and furniture

Convert the bulleted text to SmartArt

Slide 3

Layout: *Title and Content*

Title: Sports Connection Complex

Content: Insert the data file **sc complex**.

Slide 4

Layout: *Blank*

Title: None

Content: Table shown below. Use an effective design. Increase row height—especially in row 1.

Schedule of Events	
TV interview	5 a.m.
Aerobics feature	8 a.m.
Tours	9:00 – 10:45 a.m.
Dignitaries' reception	9:30 – 10:30 a.m.
Opening ceremony	11:00 – 11:45 a.m.
Picnic	12 noon
Soccer tournament	2:30 p.m.

Slide 5

Layout: *Blank*

Title: None

Content: Insert the pie chart you created in Project 2, Job 2-3 (**2-3 pie chart**). Size it to cover most of the slide below the logo.

Slide 6

Layout: *Title and Content*

Title: Printing

Content: Key the three printing expenses from **5-1 revised budget** as bulleted items and the amount spent. Convert to a Vertical Equation SmartArt graphic.

Slides 7 – 12

Layout: *Title and Content*

Content: Repeat the directions from slide 6 for each of the six remaining budget items. (Hint: After creating slide 6, insert a duplicate slide and edit it for each new budget item using the Task Pane.) Add or delete shapes if needed.

6-1 DESIGN INVITATION

- Apply creativity to design invitation.
- Print a map of the Sports Connection area.

Software: *Publisher* or *Word*

After meeting with the Grand Opening Committee, you are now ready to design the invitation to the Grand Opening ceremony. The local utility company will include the invitation and a map as inserts in the bills mailed out the month prior to the event provided that they are printed on standard-size paper. Print a map of the Sports Connection area that can also be included.

The Committee prefers a simple design; however, they told you to be creative. Both *Publisher* and *Word* samples are shown in the Quick Check below. Use the design of your preference. Add the logo to the information below if it fits in with your design. Note: The RSVP is usually formatted using left alignment, italics, and a smaller font size than the invitation. Save as **6-1 invitation**.

Information for the Invitation

Grand Opening | Sports Connection

You are cordially invited to attend | The grand opening celebration of | Sports Connection | 5600 St. Charles Avenue | Saturday, April 15, 20– Ten o'clock | Dedication ceremony | Tour of new facilities | Picnic lunch | *RSVP 555-0139*

Publisher
Use a blank sheet and add borders, objects, WordArt or other page parts for the design. The invitation templates are designed for cards only—not full sheets.

Word
Use WordArt and borders or other design objects of your choice.

Remember to use the *Sports Connection* theme.

quickcheck *Publisher* and *Word* Invitation Samples

6-1

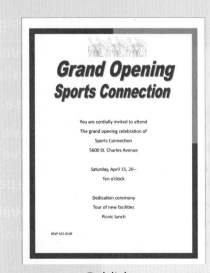

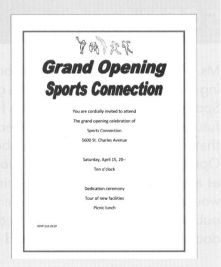

Publisher

Word

6-2 DEVELOP ARTICLE FROM OUTLINE

- Research topic using the Internet and local resources.
- Compose an article from the outline.

Software: *Word or Publisher*

Prepare an article about the benefits of participating in sports. It will be published in the local newspaper and on your website. You asked the Grand Opening Committee to suggest ideas for the article. The Committee helped you develop the title and the informal outline on the next page. Use the Internet and local resources to get additional information you need to compose the article. Follow these guidelines:

- The length of the article should be about 1 1/2 to 2 pages (at least 500 words). Write one or two paragraphs about the bulleted items in the outline.

- Use WordArt or Title style for the title.

- Include an appropriate Clip Art image near the title.

- Use heading styles as appropriate.

- Insert one or two pull quotes in the article. Use Square text wrapping.

- Create a footer with the page number and Sports Connection name and street address.

- Save the file as **6-2 sports participation**.

Use for quick comparison – your design may be quite different.   6-2

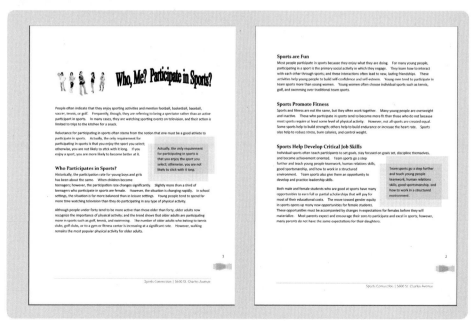

Who, Me? Participate in Sports?

- Sports are for everyone, not just the super athlete.

Who participates in sports?

- Sports are for both male and female, young and old.
- Key is to find the sports that appeal to you.

Sports are fun

- Enjoy the company of current friends.
- Meet new friends.
- Do things you enjoy doing.

Sports promote fitness

- Sports help you get in shape.
- Sports help you stay in shape.
- Sports involve exercise that relieves stress.
- Sports help with weight control.

Sports help develop critical job skills

- Sports help you develop leadership skills.
- Sports help you develop teamwork skills.

6-3 RESEARCH TRAVEL ALTERNATIVES

- Locate and compile information from websites.
- Locate hotel and flight information.
- Analyze costs.

Ms. McKay has been invited to visit the JR Sports Center located at 3730 Westheimer Road, Houston, Texas. This center is considered to be an outstanding center with a mission similar to Sports Connection's mission. She would like to use the center as a benchmark for improving and developing Sports Connection. She has asked you to locate the following information:

1. Determine the distance and driving time from the Sports Connection office to the location in Houston. If the driving time is no more than six hours, she will consider driving to save expenses.

2. Locate two or three nice (3.5–4 star ratings) hotels with rooms available for next week that are conveniently located near the center she plans to visit. Provide the name, address, and daily rate for a standard king room for each hotel.

3. If the driving time is more than eight hours, check flight schedules to determine available times and costs from New Orleans to Houston. If she flies, she plans to leave early next Monday morning and return late Tuesday evening. If she drives, she will leave next Sunday and drive back on Wednesday.

4. You decided to use your own initiative and determine what the actual savings would be if Ms. McKay drove rather than flew to Houston.
   a. The Sports Connection reimbursement rate is 42 cents per mile.
   b. Flight reimbursements are based on coach fares.
   c. Consider the cost of extra hotel nights and the $75 per diem that Sports Connection uses for meals when employees are traveling. Use the same hotel and food cost for each alternative. Estimate ground transportation costs if flight alternative is used.
   d. Add your cost analysis to the information Ms. McKay requested.

5. Design a simple and easy to read format to present the information to Ms. McKay.

6. Save as **6-3 benchmark center travel**.

6-4 DEVELOP STRATEGY FOR ADVERTISING FLYER

- Determine strategy for number of flyer versions needed.
- Determine content.
- Design and format flyer.

Software: *Word* or *Publisher*

Your instructor will tell you which software application to use. If you have access to both *Word* and *Publisher*, you may wish to prepare the flyer using both applications and then determine which one is the most effective.

Design an attractive flyer that can be posted in prominent places to announce the grand opening of Sports Connection. The flyer will be posted in a number of locations, including local businesses, government offices, schools, church recreation halls, and other public places. The purpose of the flyer is more of a reminder of the event than an invitation. Most of the people who are likely to attend have already received an invitation. Use Clip Art and make sure the print can be read from a distance.

The flyer should appeal to a number of different audiences, including:

- Young people who will participate in Sports Connection activities
- Parents who may encourage their children to participate
- Volunteers who might be willing to coach or work in other capacities
- Businesses and other organizations that may be willing to sponsor activities
- Individuals who may be willing to serve on the Advisory Council

Task 1 – Determine Best Strategy—Single Flyer or Multiple Versions

- Can one flyer appeal to all of the individuals listed above?
- Would separate flyers be more effective?

Task 2 – Make and Justify Decision

- If you choose to use one version, prepare a brief justification explaining why you think the flyer will be effective for all the groups listed.
- If you choose to prepare multiple versions, explain to whom each version is designed to appeal and why you think it will be effective.

Decision: (Select one of the following options.)

☐ **One version of flyer**

Justification: _____

_____

_____

_____

☐ **Multiple versions of flyer**

Version 1 Audience: _____

Justification: _____

_____

_____

_____

Version 2 Audience: _____

Justification: _____

_____

_____

_____

Version 3 Audience: _____

Justification: _____

_____

_____

_____

Determine the content of the flyer(s).

(Use information from the invitation—6-1.)

_____

_____

_____

_____

Format the flyer(s).

Task 3 – Determine Content

Much of the content you use will be similar to that of the invitation you prepared in Job 6–1. However, you may choose to word it differently because your purpose is different.

Task 4 – Design and Prepare Flyer

Format the flyer in an attractive, attention-getting style. Use visual enhancements such as WordArt or Clip Art or *Publisher* templates such as the colorful Company Picnic template illustrated below. If appropriate for the style, include the Sports Connection logo. Both a *Publisher* and a *Word* sample are illustrated in the Quick Check shown below. Your design may be very different from either of these illustrations. Use your own creativity to design an attention-getting flyer. Save as **6-4 flyer**.

quickcheck   *Word* and *Publisher* Illustrations   6–4 Task 4

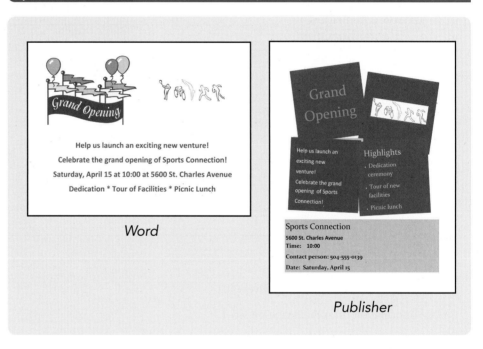

Word

Publisher

6-5 PREPARE NEWSLETTER

- Create an appealing design.
- Incorporate previously prepared materials.
- Key from handwritten source copy.
- Edit team-written articles using Comments and Track Changes.
- Condense an article to fit space available.

Software: *Publisher* or *Word*

Your instructor will tell you which software application to use. *Publisher* is recommended because of its excellent tools for creating newsletters. If you use *Publisher*, start with a blank 8.5" × 11" page in portrait orientation and create a design for future use as well.

The Grand Opening Committee recommended and Ms. McKay concurred that a newsletter be developed and sent out to a variety of individuals who have an interest in Sports Connection. The Committee suggested using Sports Connection News and Views for the first issue. They also asked that the logo be included in the newsletter. You decided to incorporate the logo in the second and third page headings.

Ms. McKay asked you to serve as editor and put together a comprehensive, three-page newsletter that will be sent to the following groups:

- Members and potential members of Sports Connection
- Volunteers and potential volunteers
- Corporate sponsors and potential sponsors
- Advisory Council

The newsletter contains a variety of short articles—some of which have been provided by other individuals, some of which you have prepared, and some of which you will create. You may position the articles in the order that best fits your design, and you may also modify the format used in these files. Include the news items listed below.

1. Message from the director (handwritten copy on page 86).
2. Mission of Sports Connection (Job 1–6).
3. Role of Advisory Council (**advisory council** data file).
4. List of Advisory Council members (Job 1–2, Task 3).
5. Articles on the importance of volunteers and corporate sponsorships (**volunteers** and **corporate sponsorships** data files).

6. Condensed version of the newspaper article (Job 6-2) you wrote. Summarize the article to be about one-third of the original length and fit in the available space. Save as **participation working file**.

Ms. McKay read the articles on volunteers and corporate sponsorships quickly. She saw an error in each article, but did not have time to make the changes in the document. Therefore, the following procedures might be helpful:

- Save data files as **volunteers working file** and **corporate sponsorships working file**.

- Proofread the articles carefully and make the corrections that are not marked.

- Accept changes indicated by Track Changes that are appropriate.

- Read the comments and implement the suggestions made by the team.

- Use the working file with the corrections made as the copy for the newsletters. Then you can simply insert the text file in your newsletter.

- Save the newsletter as **6-5 newsletter**.

Experiment and use your creativity to design an appealing newsletter. Samples for *Publisher* and *Word* are shown on the next page; however, your design may be different.

Suggestions for Word Newsletters

It is helpful to break the monotony of too much text by using visual enhancements. Examples include pull quotes, Clip Art, pictures, WordArt, shapes, and borders. You can use a text box from Shapes to help you position information easily. For example, on the *Word* banner that is illustrated on the next page the volume and date information are positioned in text boxes. The text boxes can be moved and adjusted very easily. The heading or banner illustrated on the next page was designed by using six-point lines for each of the Sports Connection theme colors used in the design. To match the lines, select the line and use CTRL plus the directional arrow to nudge it into position with the other line to form a neat corner.

Suggestions for Publisher Newsletters

Sometimes it is easier to design a template from a blank page that meets your needs rather than trying to modify a template. The illustration shown on the next page is an example of designing a template from a blank page. The Design Gallery in *Publisher 2007* and the Building Blocks in *Publisher 2010* have a number of design elements that can be used when you are beginning with a blank page. For example, the newsletter illustrated on the next page was created using the Borders heading and the Scallops pull quote. Using linked text boxes make it possible to feature more articles on the front page which gets the most attention. It is helpful to add the *Continued to and from* notices on the articles that appear on multiple pages.

quick**check**

Publisher and *Word* Illustrations; use for quick comparison—
your design may be very different.

6-5

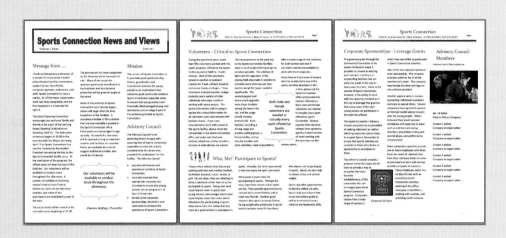

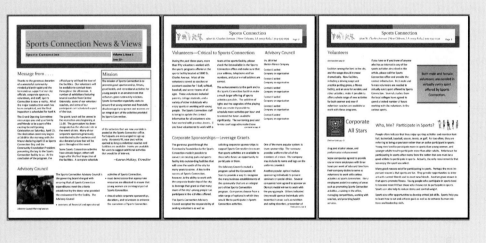

Message from. . . .

Thanks to the generous donation of a wonderful community-minded philanthropist and the tremendous support of our city officials, corporate sponsors, volunteers, and staff, Sports Connection is now a reality. All of the major construction work has been completed, and the final inspection is scheduled for April 4.

The Grand Opening Committee encourages you and your family and friends to be a part of the Grand Opening Celebration on Saturday, April 15. The dedication ceremony begins at 10:00 in the morning with the Mayor declaring April 15 as Sports Connection Day and the Community Foundation President presenting the key to the Sports Connection facility to us. At the conclusion of the program, the official party will lead the tour of the facilities. Our volunteers will be available to conduct tours throughout the afternoon. A number of exhibitions featuring several coaches from Central University, some of our volunteer coaches, and some of the participants are scheduled as part of the tour.

The picnic lunch will be served in the recreation area beginning at 11:30. The gymnasium has been designated as the alternate site in the event of rain. Many of our corporate sponsors generously contributed to the luncheon and also donated prizes that will be given throughout the event.

Some Sports Connection activities have already begun; others will begin after the final inspection of the facilities. A complete schedule of the activities that are now available is posted at the Sports Connection office. Participants are encouraged to sign up early. As events fill, new ones will be opened as long as volunteer coaches and facilities are available. Forms are available for users to suggest additional activities that would be of interest.

— Karen McKay, Director

6-6 DEVELOP A TEAMBUILDING TRAINING ACTIVITY

- Research ways to develop high-performance teams.
- Develop an activity for teambuilding.

1. Read the information below on the characteristics of high-performance teams.

2. Use keywords to search for articles and free activities on ways to build high-performance teams. Describe an activity and how to use it in training sessions for volunteers.

3. Prepare a list of five follow-up questions that teams should be asked after they complete the activity. Save the *Word* document as **6-6 teambuilding**.

Build High-Performance Teams

The success of Sports Connection is dependent on the many volunteers working effectively as a team with Sports Connection employees. Therefore, major emphasis is being placed on building high-performance teams that can get things done in the right way.

At the last staff/volunteer meeting, the group completed an exercise to determine what they believed to be the necessary characteristics of members if their teams are expected to be high-performance teams. The group came up with the following list of characteristics:

- Team members have shared goals and objectives.

- Each member focuses on attaining the team goals.

- Each member must be empowered and controls his or her own responsibilities.

- Each member is committed to the work of the team and doing his or her fair share of the work.

- Each member is given and accepts the opportunity to make decisions that affect the team.

- Each member accepts the ideas of others.

- Each member respects and trusts other members.

- Each member supports team decisions once they have been made.

For additional resources go to
www.cengage.com/keyboarding/vanhuss

Database Management

SCENARIO

The Grand Opening of the Sports Connection was a huge success. Both members and volunteers are eager to become involved. Ms. McKay asked you to invite the planners of the Grand Opening to a victory celebration to thank them personally. She also asked you to expand the database you created earlier (Job 4-1) to include members, volunteers, sports, inventory, items sold, and invoices. You will also be asked to think critically and create needed queries and reports for Ms. McKay to use in making decisions related to Sports Connection.

7-1 PREPARE MERGE LETTER AND ENVELOPES

- Use Mail Merge to prepare personalized letters and envelopes.

Software: *Word* and *Access* or *Outlook*

Task 1 – Prepare Merge Letters

The rough-draft letter on the following page needs to be finalized and set up as a main document for a mail merge. The letter will be sent to the Sports Connection Advisory Council and the Community Foundation Board of Directors.

1. Date the letter April 18. Be sure to use the Sports Connection letterhead and the Quick Part created for Ms. McKay's closing lines (Project 1). Use the recipient's first name in the salutation.

2. Select the data source as shown below.

    Contacts in Access: Select the Contacts table in the **sports connection** data base as the data source. Filter the recipients list to include the CF Directors **or** Advisory Council.

    Contacts in Outlook: Choose Select from *Outlook* Contacts and select the *CF Directors* folder. Save the main document as **7-1 main document**. Save the merged letters as **7-1 merged letters-cf**. After merging CF Directors, open the main document and select a different recipient list; select Advisory Council. Save the merged letters as **7-1 merged letters-ac**.

3. Key the letter on the following page. Save the main document as **7-1 main document**. Save the merged letters as **7-1 merged letters**. If you used *Outlook*, save as directed in Step 2.

Task 2 – Prepare Merge Envelopes

Prepare the envelopes using Mail Merge in *Word*. Use the same data source as used in preparing the letters above. Save the main document as **7-1 main document envelopes**. Save the merged envelopes as **7-1 merged envelopes**. If you used *Outlook* as the data source, save as **7-1 merged envelopes-cf** and **7-1 merged envelopes-ac**.

tips

Create Mail Merge
Mailings/Start Mail
Merge/Step by Step
Mail Merge Wizard

Dear

The grand opening of Sports Connection was a huge success thanks to
the efforts of a talented and dedicated team. The turnout for the event far
exceeded our most ambitious expectations. Perhaps the very most important
result of the event is the tremendous interest the event created in the activities of sports connection. More than a hundred potential users and volunteers
have called The Sports Connection office to request information about becoming
involved in the activities of Sports Connection.

I appreciate the excellent work you did as a team member in this successful
grand opening. Would you and your guest join us for an informal victory
celebration barbecue at my home at 2476 Broadway on Friday evening, May 5, at 7:30? The
staff of Sports Connection would like to thank you personally for playing such a
key role in the success of the Grand Opening.

Please call the Sports Connection office and let us know if you can join
us for an much-deserved evening of fellowship and relaxation. We hope you will be able to
attend.

Sincerely

Karen McKay
Director

7-2   CREATE DATABASE TABLES WITH RELATIONSHIPS

- Create new database tables.
- Import an *Excel* worksheet and *Access* table.
- Establish relationships between tables.
- Create query using two tables.
- Create report from query.

Software: *Access* and *Excel*

You need to consolidate all data into the one Sports Connection database and create new tables, forms, queries, and reports. Establishing relationships between tables is important to prevent data redundancy and reduce the risk of errors. You will work in this project and the next two projects to set up a useful database for Sports Connection.

Task 1 – Create Sports Table

Open the **sports connection** database. Create a new table named *Sports*. Create fields for *Sport*, *Type*, and *Sport Code* (primary key). Hint: For the *Type* field, use the Lookup Wizard to create a combo box that enables the user to select *Boys*, *Girls*, or *Co-ed* from a drop-down list. Enter the data shown below.

Sport	Type	Sport Code
Aerobics	Co-ed	1
Baseball	Boys	2
Basketball	Boys	3
Basketball	Girls	4
Dance	Co-ed	5
Ed. Programs	Co-ed	6
Ed. Programs	Boys	7
Ed. Programs	Girls	8
Golf	Co-ed	9
Soccer	Boys	10
Soccer	Girls	11
Softball	Girls	12
Swimming	Co-ed	13
Tennis	Boys	14
Tennis	Girls	15
Volleyball	Boys	16
Volleyball	Girls	17

tips

Import Data
External Data/Import/click
on type of data

**Create Table
Relationships
Access 2007**
Database Tools/
Show/Hide/
Relationships

Access 2010
Database Tools/
Relationships/
Relationships

Task 2 – Import External Data and Establish Relationship

1. Import the *Access* file **volunteers** from the data files into the **sports connection** database. When imported, the Volunteers table will display with the other tables in the database.

2. Import the *Excel* worksheet **exp volunteers** from the data files and append to the records in the Volunteers table just created. Sort by ID number. Key an ID number beginning at the next available number for each record missing an ID number.

3. Create a relationship between the *Sport Code* fields of the *Sports* and *Volunteers* tables. Enforce referential integrity so that a sports code will not be entered in the *Volunteers* table that does not exist in the *Sports* table.

Hint: The Quick Check below shows the *Sports* table as the "one" (1) table on the left of the Relationship pane and the *Volunteers* table as the "many" (00) table on the right. You have one sports code for each sport (Boys Soccer-10), but you will have many volunteers who may have the same sports code (Long and Patton are both volunteers for boys soccer-10).

quick**check** Check relationship between Sports and Volunteers tables. 7-2 Task 2

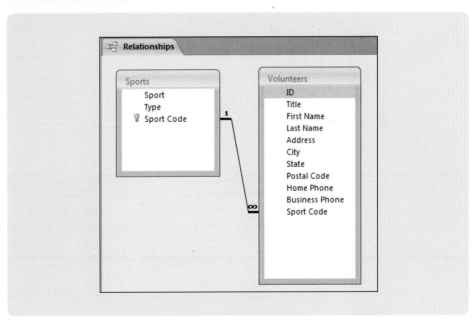

Task 3 – Create Report Using a Query

You need an attractive report showing the individuals who have volunteered for each sport, including type (boys, girls, co-ed). The report should also include home and business phone numbers.

Create Report
Create/Reports/Report
Wizard

1. Create a query to produce the data listed above. Use the *Sports* table for the *Sport* and *Type* fields; use the *Volunteers* table for *First Name, Last Name, Home Phone, Business Phone*, and *Sport Code* fields. Do not show the *Sport Code*. Save the query as *Volunteers by Sport*.

2. Use the Report Wizard to produce a report using the query you just created in Step 1. View by *Sport*, and choose the Block style and *Concourse* theme. Edit the report to enhance appearance. Save the report as *Vounteers by Sport*.

 quick**check**   Check report.   **7-2 Task 3**

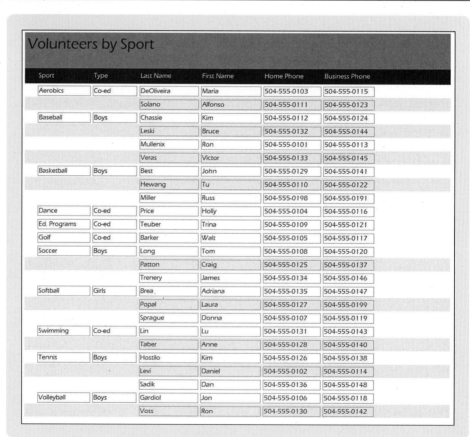

Sport	Type	Last Name	First Name	Home Phone	Business Phone
Aerobics	Co-ed	DeOliveira	Maria	504-555-0103	504-555-0115
		Solano	Alfonso	504-555-0111	504-555-0123
Baseball	Boys	Chassie	Kim	504-555-0112	504-555-0124
		Leski	Bruce	504-555-0132	504-555-0144
		Mullenix	Ron	504-555-0101	504-555-0113
		Veras	Victor	504-555-0133	504-555-0145
Basketball	Boys	Best	John	504-555-0129	504-555-0141
		Hewang	Tu	504-555-0110	504-555-0122
		Miller	Russ	504-555-0198	504-555-0191
Dance	Co-ed	Price	Holly	504-555-0104	504-555-0116
Ed. Programs	Co-ed	Teuber	Trina	504-555-0109	504-555-0121
Golf	Co-ed	Barker	Walt	504-555-0105	504-555-0117
Soccer	Boys	Long	Tom	504-555-0108	504-555-0120
		Patton	Craig	504-555-0125	504-555-0137
		Trenery	James	504-555-0134	504-555-0146
Softball	Girls	Brea	Adriana	504-555-0135	504-555-0147
		Popal	Laura	504-555-0127	504-555-0199
		Sprague	Donna	504-555-0107	504-555-0119
Swimming	Co-ed	Lin	Lu	504-555-0131	504-555-0143
		Taber	Anne	504-555-0128	504-555-0140
Tennis	Boys	Hostilo	Kim	504-555-0126	504-555-0138
		Levi	Daniel	504-555-0102	504-555-0114
		Sadik	Dan	504-555-0136	504-555-0148
Volleyball	Boys	Gardiol	Jon	504-555-0106	504-555-0118
		Voss	Ron	504-555-0130	504-555-0142

Volunteers by Sport

7-3 | CREATE DATABASE TABLE, FORM, AND REPORT

- Create new database table.
- Create form for entering data.
- Create a report from a table.

Software: Access

The next project with the database involves adding a table for members and creating a form that will be used to enter data more easily. You will also create a report of Sports Connection members.

Task 1 – Create Members Table and Form

1. Open the **sports connection** database. Create a table named *Members*. Create fields for *Member #* (primary key), *Title, Last Name, First Name, Street Address, City, State, Postal Code, Age,* and *Gender.* Hints: Enter LA as the default for the *State* field. Choose Lookup Wizard for the field type for the *Gender* field. When entering data, one will select Male or Female from a dropdown list. Set required fields as you see appropriate.

tips

Create Form
Create/Forms/Form

2. Create a form for entering data. Save the form as *Members Form.*

3. Use the form to enter the data shown on the following page.

Task 2 – Create Report of Members

Ms. McKay would like to review the members of Sports Connection by age. Create a report using the *Members* table to display age, gender, name, and city. In the Report Wizard, group by age, and sort by gender and then by last name. Use the Stepped layout and Concourse design. Save as *Members by Age.*

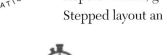

Check report design by viewing this partial report.   **7-3 Task 2**

Age	Gender	Last Name	First Name	City
16				
	Female	Riley	Julia	Metairie
	Female	Salvas	Maria	Metairie
	Male	Bell	Boyd	New Orleans
17				
	Female	Garcia	Ana	New Orleans
	Female	Quinn	Betty	New Orleans

First & Last Name		Address	*City	Postal Code	Age	Gender
Lee	Bader	501 Norton Ave.	New Orleans	70123-1123	17	Male
Bill	Ayers	66 Stutz Dr.	New Orleans	70126-2226	21	Male
Gail	Barto	201 Taft Place	New Orleans	70119-3319	19	Female
Brian	Luke	345 Marion Ave.	Metairie	70005-2355	17	Male
Julia	Riley	2221 Nora St.	Metairie	70003-5533	16	Female
Ben	Mabry	448 Seine St.	New Orleans	70114-1114	19	Male
Ann	Patel	608 Pope St.	New Orleans	70121-0021	18	Female
Steve	Drury	558 Airline Hwy.	Kenner	70062-0062	20	Male
John	Reese	702 Elder St.	New Orleans	70122-2322	17	Male
Betty	Quinn	388 Eton St.	New Orleans	70114-1114	17	Female
Maria	Salvas	4409 Mandarin St.	Metairie	70005-0005	16	Female
David	Ryan	3389 Jefferson Blvd.	Kenner	70062-1162	20	Male
Jose	Mendez	4306 Jefferson Blvd.	Kenner	70062-3362	21	Male
Po-Ling	Wong	402 Utica St.	Metairie	70002-4622	18	Female
Paul	Fogle	88 Sage St.	New Orleans	70122-4322	19	Male
Te-Long	Wang	601 Toulon St.	New Orleans	70129-6629	18	Male
Boyd	Bell	2907 Poydras St.	New Orleans	70113-2213	16	Male
Ana	Garcia	4089 Slidell St.	New Orleans	70114-1314	17	Female
Phill	Asbill	2288 Clarke St.	Metairie	70002-0202	19	Male
Lesa	Berry	706 Georgia St.	Metairie	70005-3355	22	Female
Ramon	Arvay	3310 Flagler St.	Metairie	70003-1011	20	Male
Melvin	Norton	2206 Audubon Blvd.	New Orleans	70125-2206	18	Male
Anne	Pace	2766 Baronne St.	New Orleans	70113-3343	19	Female
Don	Pruitt	540 Basin St.	New Orleans	70112-4412	22	Male
Patsy	Phyall	806 Bourbon St.	New Orleans	70116-8806	21	Female

*Note: All cities are in Louisiana.

7-4 USE DATABASE FOR DECISION MAKING

- Import database tables and establish relationships.
- Create queries to answer questions.
- Create reports for decision making.

Software: *Access* and *PowerPoint*

Task 1 – Import External Data and Establish Relationships

1. Open the **sports connection** database. Import the *Access* file **sales** from the data files. When imported, the *Inventory, Items Sold*, and *Invoice* tables will display with the other tables in the database. Browse the tables in Datasheet View and Design View to become familiar with the data in the tables. Close the tables.

2. Create the following relationships and enforce referential integrity for each:
   a. Part # in the *Inventory* table and Part # in the *Items Sold* table.
   b. Invoice # in the *Invoice* table and Invoice # in the *Items Sold* table.
   c. Member # in the *Members* table and Member # in the *Invoice* table.

   Hint: The "one" table is listed first in the list above and the "many" table is listed second. Remember you have one Part # in the *Inventory* table and many parts being listed in the *Items Sold* table. You have one invoice number in the *Invoice* table and many invoice numbers in the *Items Sold* table because you hope an invoice includes more than one item sold. You have one Member # in the *Members* table and hopefully the same member requesting many invoices.

Task 2 – Create Queries

Ms. McKay has requested you create three queries to use to access information quickly. Create the queries and save as indicated.

1. A member asks, "Which invoices do I owe and what are the amounts?" Include the following fields: *Member #, First Name, Last Name* (*Members* table), *Invoice #* (*Items Sold* table), and *Date* (*Invoice* table). The last field is a calculated field to compute the total of each invoice. Key the field as follows: **Total: [quantity]*[actual price]**. Test the query by entering the last name **Bader** in the criteria row. Run the query to display Bader's invoices. See the design grid below to check your query design. Save as *Invoices Inquiry*.

Sidebar

21st Century Skills
INNOVATION

tips

Import Data
External Data/Import/click on type of data

Create Table Relationships
Access 2007
Database Tools/Show/Hide/Relationships

Access 2010
Database Tools/Relationships/Relationships

quickcheck   Check the query design.

Field:	Member #	First Name	Last Name	Invoice #	Date	Total: [quantity]*[actual price]
Table:	Members	Members	Members	Items Sold	Invoice	
Total:	Group By	Group By	Group By	Group By	Group By	Sum
Sort:						
Show:	☑	☑	☑	☑	☑	☑
Criteria:			"Bader"			
or:						

2.   Ms. McKay asks, "What are the number of passes sold and their breakdown?" Decide which fields you will need from which table/s. What criterion is needed to answer this question? Save as *Quantity Sold by Inventory Category*.

3.   You write a question that would provide helpful information. Use any of the tables in the database. Create the query and save as *7-4 Task 2 My Inquiry*.

Task 3 – Create a Report from a Query

Ms. McKay would like to review a report that shows sales by item. You must first create the query and then the report.

1.   Create the query with the following fields: *Part # (Items Sold* table), *Description (Invoice* table) and *Period, Access, Level,* and *Category (Inventory* table). Key **Total** as a new field with the following formula: **Total: [quantity] * [actual price]**. Click Totals to show the Group by row and select Sum. Position the *Total* field as the second field in the query. Save as *Sales by Item*.

2.   Create a report using the query created above. In the Report Wizard, group by Category and sort by Part #. Under Summary Options, choose Sum. Choose the Block layout and Concourse design. Size fields appropriately and format amounts as currency and no decimal places. Save as *Sales by Item*.

Task 4 – Compose a Memo Analyzing the Report Data

Analyze the report created in Task 3 carefully and answer the following questions. Add two more questions of your own to the list. Compose a memo to Ms. McKay answering these questions. Save as **7-4 memo**.

1.   What is the total revenue for the invoices in the database?

2.   What is the amount of revenue received from the following categories?
     a.   Classes
     b.   Special Services
     c.   Passes

3.   Are the three levels of swimming classes being requested? Explain.

4.   Is the daycare service being requested? Explain.

Task 5 – Create a Report

Using the data in the **sports connection** database, create a report that you would consider helpful to Ms. McKay as she makes decisions. If a query is needed, save it as *7-4 Task 5 Query*. Save the report as *7-4 Task 5 Your Report*.

Task 6 – Recommend Best Query and Report

Although Sports Connection is new and just receiving customer orders, Ms. McKay was wise in asking you to develop queries and reports that can be reviewed daily and/or weekly. Ms. McKay will make effective management decisions using these well-designed queries and reports.

1. Select a team of three to five students. Ask each team member to share the queries created in Tasks 4 and 5 and the report created in Task 5.

2. Select the query and report that represents the best work completed by members of your team and one that Ms. McKay would definitely find useful.

3. Prepare a *PowerPoint* presentation that includes a title slide with the names of the team members. Create slides to display the query (design grid and results) and report. Be prepared to explain their use in making a decision. Save the presentation as **7-4 sample best query and report**.

Create Screen Capture
Display query or report. Press Alt+Print Screen. Paste the image where desired. Crop and size appropriately.

Draw Conclusions

Sound judgment is the ability to consider evidence and make the right decision and is essential for success in our personal lives and in the workplace. The decision-making model presented in Project 1 is a systematic method to follow when making sound decisions. As one digs deeper in understanding decision making, one might ask the question, "Is there a formula for drawing a conclusion?"

To draw a conclusion, first look at the information in the scenario/problem. Are there connections between any of the pieces? Think about past experiences and consider if those experiences apply to this situation. Consider information that may not be directly stated in the scenario. Finally, use all of the information you know to draw the conclusion.

7-5   PREPARE MEMO AND LABELS FROM DATABASE

- Prepare memo.
- Prepare mailing labels from database.

Software: *Word* and *Access*

Task 1 – Prepare Memo

Ms. McKay drafted the memo on the following page to be sent to all registered users of Sports Connection concerning the fee schedule the Advisory Council approved at its last meeting. Send a copy of the memo to the Advisory Council and attach the fee schedule created in Project 2 (2-4). Key **Fee Structure** as the subject. Save as **7-5 memo**.

Task 2 – Prepare Mailing Labels from Access

Prepare mailing labels for the registered members of Sports Connection.

1. Open the **sports connection** database. Create the mailing labels using the Report object.

Create Labels
Create/Reports/Labels

2. Use *English* for the Unit of Measure and Avery 6460, 1" × 2 5/8" labels. Change the font to Calibri and sort by the *Postal Code*.

3. Save the report as *Mailing Labels for Members*.

Several members have asked questions about the Sports Connection fee schedule; therefore, I am providing each registered Member of Sports Connection with information about the process of setting fees and with a copy of the current fee schedule.

Criteria for the gift to establish Sports Connection specified that the Advisory Council is responsible for overseeing the financial operation of Sports Connection. This responsibility includes securing additional funds to enhance the operations and ensuring that young people who are financially disadvantaged (as determined by the Community Foundation Guidelines) have access to all activities of Sports Connection at no charge. Community Foundation Guidelines are posted in the office and are also available directly from the Community Foundation.

The Sports Connection Advisory Council has established the following guides for fees:

- Financially disadvantaged youth receive passes that provide complete access, and they pay no fees whatsoever.

- Fees are not charged for use of the park; the soccer, baseball, and softball fields; the basketball, volleyball, and tennis courts; aerobics and dance classes; or for educational programs.

- Fees will be charged for access passes to the swimming pool, driving range, locker rooms, and to the equipment in the fitness center.

- Fees may be paid for access passes on a daily, weekly, or monthly basis. Passes are available for individual activities or at a reduced rate for access to all activities.

- The Sports Connection Advisory Council reviews fees and may change them at its fall meeting.

Attachment: Fee schedule

7-6 DESIGN ANNOUNCEMENT AND PREPARE LABELS

- Design an announcement.
- Query database.
- Print labels from query.

Software: *Access, Word,* or *Publisher*

Task 1 – Design an Announcement

Use the information on the following page to prepare an announcement of an upcoming Junior Golf Clinic. Spell out all abbreviations. The clinic is designed to introduce young girls and boys to the basics of golf. Sports Connection is making a conscious effort to get more girls involved in sports, especially golf and tennis.

Use your creativity in formatting the announcement in either *Word* or *Publisher*. However, use WordArt to format the announcement title, use Clip Art that would be appropriate for golf, and list the two sponsors at the bottom of the announcement (Sports Connection and Central University) with their logos. Locate a Clip Art image of an eagle for the Central University logo. Hint: See RGB numbers in *Sports Connection* theme to choose accent colors in the *Publisher* flyer. Save as **7-6 announcement**.

What:	The Junior Golf Clinic is a Special event for girls and boys who are 17 years old or younger who would like to learn how to play golf.
When:	Sat. morn, april 6, from 8:30–11:30
Where:	The S C practice putting and Driving Range
General Information:	Call the S C office (555-0139) to register no later than Th, april 5, at 4:30 p.m. No prior golf knowledge is required. Golf clubs will be provided if you do not own golf clubs. Golf access passes are not required for this special event.
	Young girls are especially encouraged to learn to play golf. Many business contacts are made on golf courses. In addition to being fun, golf provided an excellent opportunity to network with managers, customers, and clients. Informal networking is a key way to enhance your career.
Presented by:	Women and Men's Golf Coaches and Teams Central University Eagles

quickcheck · Sample *Word* and *Publisher* announcements · 7-6 Task 1

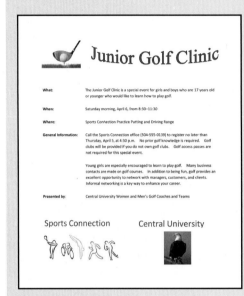

Publisher Sample

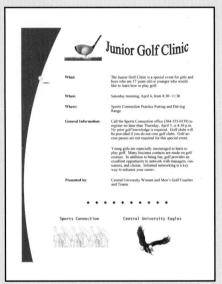

Word Sample

Task 2 – Create Query

You are mailing the announcement created above to all members who are under 18 years old. Open the **sports connection** database and create a query to identify these members. Sort by *Postal Code*. Save as *Members Under 18*.

Task 3 – Prepare Mailing Labels

From the *Access* database, prepare mailing labels using the query created in Task 2 for members under 18 years old. Save labels as *Labels Members Under 18*.

7-7   DEVELOP HANDOUT AND LABELS

- Prepare handouts for seminars.
- Research and summarize information.
- Query database and print labels.

Software: *Access, Word,* and *Internet*

Task 1 – Prepare Handout

Ms. McKay has asked you to develop an attractive handout to be distributed during a seminar entitled "Enjoy a Healthy Lifestyle." You can use the sample copy on the following page as a basis for the handout's text. Ms. McKay's objective is to use the same format for all seminar handouts. With this objective in mind, consider various design elements that would be attractive and useful for the seminar participants. Ideas for your consideration are attractive layout, custom headers and footers, relevant Clip Art or photographs, pull quotes, sidebars, WordArt, SmartArt, and drop caps. You will want to consider how you can promote Sports Connection services and its image (logo and themes).

Include the names of the four recreational supervisors on the handout. Create a query in *Access* to find these names; save as *Recreational Supervisors*. Copy and paste the query results in the handout. Edit attractively and appropriately. See the Quick Check for a sample. Save as **7-7 handout**.

Task 2 – Create Query and File Folder Labels

You have been asked to prepare labeled file folders for members of Sports Connection who will be attending an upcoming seminar.

1. Open the **sports connection** database and create a query to identify male members. Sort in ascending order by last name. Save as *Male Members*.

2. From the *Access* database, prepare the file folder labels (Avery Index Maker 3) using the query created above Save labels as *Labels Male Members*.

Repeat steps 1-2 and prepare file folder labels for all female members. Save the query and labels appropriately.

Although young people are more likely to die or be severely injured in automobile or work accidents and violent assaults involving alcohol or drugs than from illnesses, living a healthy lifestyle is still very important. It is important for young people because living a healthy lifestyle is the key to looking, feeling, and doing your best.

What is a Healthy Lifestyle?

Living a healthy lifestyle does not mean giving up everything that is fun. It does mean that you must make wise choices in a variety of areas including diet, weight control, exercise, use of tobacco, alcohol, and drugs, and taking preventive measures to avoid accidents and diseases. Physical fitness results from living a healthy lifestyle.

Fitness Evaluation

Sports Connection has arranged to make a comprehensive fitness evaluation available to users of the Fitness Center and aerobics classes. Graduate and undergraduate student interns in the Exercise Science Department of Central University can administer an evaluation of your current fitness level for a nominal fee of $20. The evaluation includes:

- Resting heart rate and blood pressure
- Height, weight, and body (fat) composition
- Flexibility
- Muscular strength and endurance
- Cardiorespiratory fitness
- Cholesterol screening
- Dietary analysis
- Nutritional counseling
- Personalized exercise program

Comparable evaluations at local health clubs cost $50 to $100. The program is supervised by Dr. Lynn Massa, head of the Exercise Science Department.

Diet and Weight Control

A healthy diet refers to both the selection and the quantity of food. A low fat, low sodium, low sugar diet is ideal. For most young people, the best advice is to eat a variety of foods including vegetables, fruits, and grain products. Studies show that more than 20 percent of teenage boys and girls are overweight. A small, but growing percentage of teenage girls with a desire to be extremely thin develops severe eating disorders such as anorexia nervosa or bulimia nervosa. Excessive dieting and exercise lead to major health and emotional problems.

Exercise

An appropriate exercise program is critical for physical fitness. To be effective, an exercise program must include a cardiovascular workout as well as muscular strength and endurance workouts. A good workout should include at least 20 minutes of exercise three times a week. Combining a good exercise program and a healthy diet provides effective weight control.

Smoking, Alcohol, and Drugs

Smoking, alcohol, and illegal drugs have severe health consequences as well as severe consequences on physical performance. In some cases, athletes foolishly take drugs (amphetamines and steroids) to enhance performance for a period of time, but they do irreparable harm to their health.

Other Preventive Measures

A healthy lifestyle requires preventive as well as proactive measures. Driving is a good example of an area where preventive measures are extremely important since accidents are a primary cause of deaths of young people.

Sample Word handout

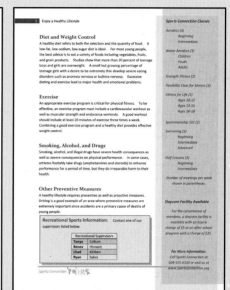

Note use of drop cap, WordArt, Clip Art, pull quote, SmartArt, and heading style.

Note use of header, footer with logo, and sidebar with Sports Connection services.

For additional resources go to
www.cengage.com/keyboarding/vanhuss

PROJECT 8

Program Management

SCENARIO

In this project, you will focus on managing programs efficiently and effectively. A SharePoint site has been developed to facilitate communicating with volunteers and members. Attractive documents that do not require special web formatting can be posted on the site to attract the attention of volunteers and members. You will save all documents for SharePoint in your solutions file; Molly (receptionist) will post all documents for the staff. In addition, you will manage the search for a full-time coordinator to schedule and coordinate sports programs.

8-1 DESIGN MEMBERSHIP APPLICATION

- Design a form and prepare it for printing.

Sports Connection needs an attractive application form to place in local schools and businesses for prospective members. The leadership team decided the information on the next page must be included. Potential members will handwrite the information on the form, but it should be designed so it is easy to enter data from the form into the *Members* table in the Sports Connection database. A sample is shown below to provide ideas, but your form should be original.

1. Format the form using narrow margins so that it will fit on one page.

2. Include the Sports Connection logo on the form.

3. Use WordArt to feature the Sports Connection name. Position the address and telephone number in a text box below the name.

4. Center the names of the three sections of the form and use shading to separate the heading from the application information. All three headings should have the same format and should fit on one line.

5. Use text boxes for the information that is to be handwritten on the form.

6. Use tables for the types of passes and the sports participation information. Position the columns as shown below to ensure the form fits on one page. List the ten sports now offered at Sports Connection, plus "educational programs," and leave spaces for additional sports to be added.

7. Save as **8-1 application**.

Text Boxes
Insert/Illustrations/
Shape/Draw Text
Box **or** Insert/Text/Text
Box/Draw Text Box

Use text boxes to position information on the form.

Use tables to simplify the tabular information.

Remember to use Sports Connection theme colors and font scheme.

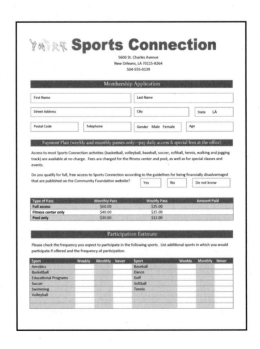

Logo   *Sports Connection* -(use WordArt)

Address and Telephone Number

(Use solid fill)

Membership Application

Add required user information:

First Name	Last Name		
Street Address	City	State	LA
Postal Code	Telephone Number	Gender Male Female	Age

Payment Plan (weekly and monthly passes only–pay daily access and special fees at the office)

Access to most Sports Connection activities (basketball, volleyball, baseball, soccer, softball, tennis, walking and jogging track) is available at no charge. Fees are charged for the fitness center and pool, as well as for special classes and events.

Do you qualify for full, free access to Sports Connection according to the guidelines for being financially disadvantaged that are published on the Community Foundation website? Yes No Do not know

Type of Pass	Monthly Pass	Weekly Pass	Amount Paid
Full access	$60.00	$25.00	
Fitness center only	$40.00	$15.00	
Pool only	$30.00	$12.00	

Participation Estimate

Please check the frequency you expect to participate in the following sports. List additional sports in which you would participate if offered and the frequency of participation.

(Create an eight-column table. Use the following headings in the first four columns: Sports, Weekly, Monthly, and Never; then repeat the headings in the second group of four columns. Under the two Sports columns, list the 10 sports, plus "Educational Programs," offered in alphabetical order as you tab across columns. Leave the other columns blank for applicant to check. Add two to five blank rows for applicant to write in additional sports they would like to see offered. This table format is used to ensure that the form fits on one page.)

8-2   PREPARE DOCUMENTS FOR SHAREPOINT SITE

- Rename document for posting.
- Compose memo to members.
- Analyze results and format worksheet.

Software: *Word* and *Excel*

Sports Connection recently created a SharePoint site that is to be used for posting information for members and volunteers. SharePoint is a Microsoft server that makes it easy to share documents and for members to collaborate on projects. Ms. McKay and the leadership team discussed the types of documents that will be helpful to post for members. The group decided to start by posting newsletters, tips for improving performance in the various sports, and the application you prepared in the previous job. She asked you to manage the SharePoint site. Members will only be able to read information such as the calendar events posted and the documents that you wish to share with them. They can also download the documents as shown in the screen below. Members have been given a demonstration on how to use the SharePoint site and a set of directions to follow in case they need help.

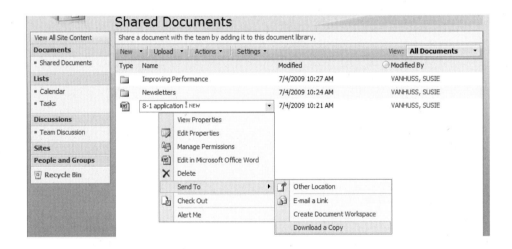

Task 1 – Rename Document for Posting

After reviewing the documents posted on the SharePoint site (shown on the screen above), you decided that the name used for the membership application might not be meaningful to members. Open **8-1 application** from your solutions and save it as **sports connection application**. Since you want to maintain a copy of the document with the original name and also have one with a different name for the SharePoint site, you chose to use the Save As command rather than the Rename command. Molly will delete the document on the site and post this one.

Task 2 – Compose Memo to Members

Compose a memo (or an e-mail if available) to all Sports Connection members and remind them to check the SharePoint site frequently. Also ask them to download the Sports Connection Application and give it to their friends and encourage them to become members of Sports Connection. Save as **8-2 memo**.

Task 3 – Analyze Results and Format Spreadsheet

You used the new website polling feature to survey youth between the ages of 8 and 21 about their interest in participating in sports. The survey was widely publicized by the local newspaper, by local schools, and by newsletters. The results of the survey are included in the *Excel* survey data file.

You decided that the following information would be of interest:

- Who participated (by gender, age categories, and whether they were members)

- Of the current sports offered, which were the most desired by youth

- What new sports were of particular interest to the youth

The *Excel* worksheet will be posted on the SharePoint site. Complete and format Sheet1 of the survey data file as directed below. Limit the sheet to one page.

1. Add the totals in the columns and rows where indicated.

2. Format the title of the sheet using Cell Styles Title; change font color to white.

3. Format the column heads using Cell Styles Heading 1; right-align headings over the three columns with numbers.

4. Format each of the major categories: *Responses, Sports Connection Membership, Age Categories, Team Sports Offered Rankings*, etc., using Cell Styles 60% – Accent 1.

5. Change margins to .5" top and bottom. Center the sheet horizontally on the page.

6. Save as **8-2 survey results**.

The leadership team analyzed the data, compared it to current member data, and made the following notes:

- The percentage of youth in the survey matches very closely the profile of the current Sports Connection members in both gender and age categories.

- The most popular team sports with current members are soccer and basketball. This is true of both male and female members.

- For current members, tennis and swimming are the most popular individual sports for both males and female. Golf ranks second for males and third for females.

- Most of the current members play at least two sports.

- Current members prefer track and field events to walking and jogging.

tips

Cell Styles
Home/Styles/Cell Styles
Select the cell to be formatted and apply desired style.

Center Sheet on Page
Page Layout/Page Setup/Margins/Custom Margins
Center sheet on page horizontally.

8-3 | CREATE GRAPHICS AND PRESENTATION

- Prepare graphics from the worksheet data.
- Prepare a *PowerPoint* presentation.

Software: *Excel* and *PowerPoint*

Task 1 – Prepare Graphics for Presentation

You will use the information in the worksheet you completed in Job 8-2 to prepare graphics to present the information more effectively in a *PowerPoint* presentation.

- Use your judgment to determine which information you will present graphically—not all information has to be presented graphically—and what type of chart would be most appropriate to use.

- Prepare each chart in a new worksheet. Add an appropriate title and where appropriate show values and percentages. Name each sheet with a short name to identify the graphic it contains. Be creative in formatting the graphics. Save as **8-3 graphics**.

Task 2 – Prepare PowerPoint Presentation

Prepare a *PowerPoint* presentation with at least six slides to present the results of the survey effectively, using both graphics and text. See the illustration on the next page. Use the illustration for ideas; do not try to make your solution look like the one illustrated. Be creative in developing and presenting the information effectively. Remember that your audience will consist of the Advisory Council, potential sponsors, parents, and potential members.

- Use an appropriate title slide.

- Use the leadership team's analytical notes from Job 8-2 to add text to slides.

- Use appropriate transitions and animations for your audience.

- Use the last slide or two to present conclusions or recommendations about the data, explaining what the data means and what you might be able to do with it. You can address the conclusions or recommendations from any of several perspectives—what additional sports should be offered, the need for sponsorships to expand offerings, or a campaign to attract these potential members who have an obvious interest in sports. Make sure the conclusions and recommendations are consistent with the survey responses.

- Save as **8-3 presentation**.

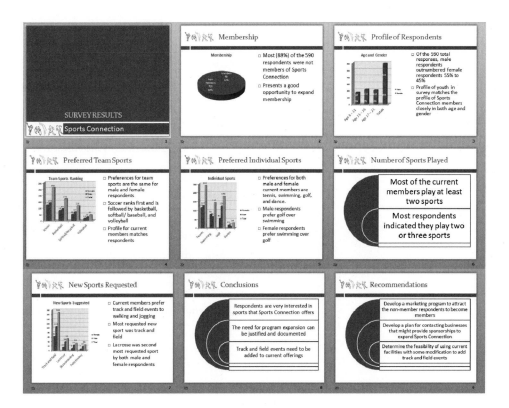

8-3 Task 2

Check your presentation to ensure that you:
✓ Used appropriate charts that accurately represent the information you are presenting.
✓ Selected relevant points from the team's analytical notes to add appropriate text to each slide to explain the data or highlight important points.
✓ Based your conclusions and recommendations on the data from the survey and that they are logical.

8-4   PREPARE EMPLOYMENT ANNOUNCEMENT

- Prepare an employment announcement.

Software: *Publisher* or *Word*

Ms. McKay has approved a new position for a full-time sports coordinator. She has asked you to coordinate the search. Information about the position has been posted on the Sports Connection website (www.SportsConnection.org). Prepare an announcement for the SharePoint site as some of the volunteers may be good candidates for this position.

Format the announcement using the information shown on page 118. Your instructor may direct you to use either *Publisher* or *Word* for this job. If not, select the application that you believe would produce the most attractive one-page document. Consider the following points:

- Include the Sports Connection name and logo in a prominent position.

- If you use *Publisher*, start with a blank 8.5"×11" sheet and add graphic elements to the publication.

- If you use *Word*, use WordArt and text boxes to manage blocks of information easily.

- Add below e-mail address: For information, visit the Sports Connection website: www.sportsconnection.org.

- Save as **8-4 announcement**.

quickcheck **Your solution may vary significantly from these illustrations.**

8-4

Publisher

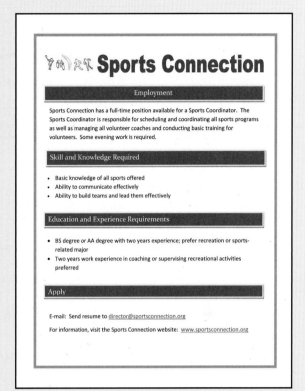

Word

Employment

Sports Connection has a full-time position available for a Sports Coordinator. The Sports Coordinator is responsible for scheduling and coordinating all sports programs as well as managing all volunteer coaches and conducting basic training for volunteers. Some evening work is required.

Skills and Knowledge Required

- Basic knowledge of all sports offered.
- Ability to communicate effectively.
- Ability to build teams and lead them effectively.

Educational and Experience Requirements

- BS degree or AA degree with two years experience; prefer recreation or sports-related major.
- Two years work experience in coaching or supervising recreational activities preferred.

Apply

E-Mail: Send resume to director@sportsconnection.org.

8-5 DEVELOP INTERVIEW GUIDE

- Research effective interview questions.
- Apply Sports Connection decision-making model.
- Develop effective interview questions.

You have asked the leadership team to help you review the résumés of all candidates for the new Sports Coordinator position. The team will select and interview six candidates. The first interview will be used to narrow the search to three finalists who will return for a second interview. Ms. McKay will participate in the second interview.

1. Read the information below and then use the Internet and local resources to locate and read at least three or four credible articles on effective interview questions. Think carefully about how you will decide who can do the job most effectively.

2. Then write ten questions that each of the six candidates will be asked during the interview process. Make sure that at least three or four of the questions are behavioral-type questions. Ask your team (three classmates) to critique the questions.

3. Leave space after each question for notes during the interview.

4. Save as **8-5 interview guide**.

Make Judgments and Decisions

One of the most important decisions organizations must make is hiring the right individual for a particular position. Decisions are only as good as the information on which they are based. Therefore, it is critical to collect both the right type of information and an adequate amount of information on which to base decisions.

Research shows that most interviews are not effective because people often make decisions in the first five minutes of the interview and base the decision on first impressions rather than on adequate, objective data. Behavioral questions tend to produce better data in an interview than other types of questions. Behavioral questions require candidates to describe what they have done or would do in a particular situation that occurred on the job. For example, a behavioral question might be: Tell us how you would handle the situation if five or six irate parents came to see you with complaints about a particular coach not giving their children a fair amount of playing time on a sports team for 8- to 10-year-old children. Behavioral questions may also provide insights on a person's character or ethical standards.

8-6 RESEARCH TOPIC AND PREPARE PRESENTATION

- Research topic.
- Prepare *PowerPoint* presentation.

Software: *PowerPoint* and *Word*

Each week a presentation providing tips on improving performance in a particular sport will be featured on the SharePoint site.

Your task is to:

1. Select a sport you would like to learn more about.

2. Use the Internet or local resources to research ways to improve performance in that sport. Obtain information from a minimum of three different sources.

3. Use *Word's* thesaurus to help you find creative words for your presentation.

4. Prepare a *PowerPoint* presentation to provide tips on improving performance in that particular sport.

5. Use the standard Sports Connection design. Prepare at least six slides.

6. Use a variety of slide layouts and avoid all text slides. Add SmartArt or Clip Art as appropriate.

7. This presentation is designed for members. Choose transitions and animations with that in mind.

8. Save as **8-6 (name of sport) tips**.

8-7 PREPARE A GOLF ANNOUNCEMENT

- Create an attention-getting design.
- Prepare an announcement about a golf opportunity.

Software: *Publisher* or *Word*

A major corporate sponsor has made it possible for members of Sports Connection to play golf at a local course. Be creative as you use the information below to prepare the announcement that will be posted on the SharePoint site for all members. Use colorful WordArt and golf scenes from Clip Art. Save as **8-7 golf announcement**.

Golf Opportunity

Major corporate sponsor makes it possible for members of Sports Connection to have an opportunity to play golf

River Course

Sunnyside Golf Club

Mondays through Thursdays

8:00 a.m. to 1:00 p.m.

Nominal charge of $12 per person

For free access members, six free passes are available per day—a priority system has been developed to ensure that all eligible members have an opportunity to play golf

8-8 ENHANCE EMPLOYEE DEVELOPMENT

- Help employees understand the value of having a positive attitude.
- Help employees and volunteers improve their attitudes.

1. Read the information shown below.

2. Search the Internet for articles on developing a positive attitude and come up with a list of ten benefits of having a positive attitude. Save the list as **8-8 benefits**.

3. Prepare a list of ten things that a person can do to improve his or her work attitude.

4. Save as **8-8 positive attitude**.

Positive Attitude

When employers are asked to list the characteristics of successful people in their organizations, they usually include *having a positive attitude* in the top five characteristics on their list. When they are hiring people, they also list *having a positive attitude* as one of the top characteristics they seek. Yet in the interview process, it is very difficult to determine if the individual you are considering hiring will be described by their peers as a person with a positive attitude. Leaders are responsible for helping employees develop attitudes that enhance performance.

Self-confidence is very closely linked to having a positive attitude. Many people describe self-confidence as a self-fulfilling prophecy. If you think you can do something, you are quite likely to do it. If you do not think you can do something and have doubts about your ability, you are not likely to do things you are capable of doing very well. Workers with a poor self-image are more likely to look for faults than strengths. They often think of themselves as failures if they fail on one little thing rather than having the attitude of "that did not work and I need to try something else to find something that will work."

People with positive attitudes tend to smile more and to be more optimistic; however, that does not mean that they have to be "rah rah cheerleaders!" It means they approach problems as challenges that also come with opportunities and try to think of ways to solve them.

For additional resources go to
www.cengage.com/keyboarding/vanhuss

Program Connectivity

SCENARIO

The leadership group discussed the possibility of using social media tools to promote Sports Connection. Ms. McKay asked that a team explore this possibility. First, the team must read credible research on how non-profit organizations are using social media to market themselves. Then, they should visit selected sites and determine their appropriateness for Sports Connection. The team will develop a plan for using social media to supplement the traditional marketing plan. Finally, the team will prepare a presentation with a handout, and deliver the presentation to the Advisory Council.

9-1 Visit Social Media Sites and Collect Information

9-2 Determine Applicability of Each Site

9-3 Create Social Media Plan

9-4 Prepare and Deliver Presentation

9-5 Evaluate Your Team

9-1 VISIT SOCIAL MEDIA SITES AND COLLECT INFORMATION

- Interact effectively with team members.
- Determine the sites the team will visit.
- Decide the type of information needed.
- Collect the information.

Software: *Word*

Your instructor will appoint teams of three or four people to work on this project. Each team will determine how members of the team will interact and who will do the various tasks that need to be done. Team members will likely have some experience using social media; however, they are not likely to be familiar with the ways in which non-profit organizations, such as Sports Connection, might use social media effectively for marketing and promotional purposes.

You know from the budgets that you have prepared that only the Grand Opening had funds allocated for marketing. Any expenditures for marketing and promotion other than for the Grand Opening would have to come out of a very limited budget for operating expenses. Therefore, you would need to work with commercial social networks rather than trying to build a network on the Sports Connection website. For a good reference to provide background information, check www.nonprofitsocialnetworksurvey.com. The primary cost of using a commercial social network is staff time.

Task 1 – Learn About Social Media Tools Used for Non-Profit Marketing

1. Read the information on social media tools on page 126.

2. Search the Internet using the keywords *social networks for non-profit marketing*, and read at least three articles on the topic.

3. Use a title such as *Social Media Articles* and key the following information about each article:
   a. Name of the article, the author, and the date of the article
   b. The URL for the website
   c. Would you recommend the article to team members—yes or no? Why or why not?
   d. Save as **9-1 social media articles**.

Task 2 – Visit Social Media Sites and Collect Information

Team members should take the following steps to complete this task:

1. Spend a few minutes discussing the articles read prior to visiting the sites.

2. Visit different social media sites. Determine how to ensure coverage of all types of social media described on the next page and multiple sites of each type when appropriate.

3. Develop a form for collecting information that includes the following: name, type of site, URL, a brief description of the site visited, a list of the key advantages of using the site, a list of the key disadvantages of using the site, the cost for using the site if any, general comments, the team member's name, and the date the site was visited. Design the form so that it is easy to fill in using *Word*. One illustration is shown in the Quick Check below. (Hint: Do not draw lines; leave blank spaces for information to be added.)

4. Save the form as a template named **social media form**.

5. Complete a separate form for each site visited. Save the completed forms as **9-1** *plus the name of the site* (such as **9-1 facebook**).

quickcheck   The design of your form may be different.   9-1 Task 2

Social Media Site Visit Report

Site Information
Name of site:

Type of site:

Site URL:

Description of Site

Advantages of Using the Site

Disadvantages of Using the Site

Costs for Using the Site, If Any

General Comments

Team Member Visiting the Site
Name:

Date site was visited:

Understand and Utilize Appropriate Social Media

Non-profit organizations use a variety of commercial social media tools to promote or market themselves at a relatively low cost. Some sites may fit in more than one category. The primary cost is the staff time allocated to working on these networks. Most non-profit organizations find that marketing is more effective when social media tools are used in combination with traditional promotion and marketing tools.

Social Media Tools

The categories or groups listed below are one way of looking at different options available. Many other approaches can be used to organize or analyze social media tools.

Social networks are generally thought of as tools for sharing information with an online community of people with common interests. Facebook, LinkedIn, and MySpace are examples of frequently used social networks.

Micro-blogging sites enable users to send brief messages (often 140 characters or less) to a group of people which in turn can be sent to other groups. Twitter and Tumblr are examples of micro-blogging sites.

Video sharing sites provide a platform for people to post videos to share with others. YouTube, Metacafe, Break, and Google Video are examples of video-sharing sites.

Photo sharing sites provide a platform for people to post photographs to share with others. Examples include Flickr, Photobucket, Webshots, and Fotki.

Blogs are sites that provide publishing tools for people to post articles and various types of information to share with others and accept comments from readers. Examples of blog hosting sites include Blogger from Google, WordPress, and Live Journal.

Bookmarking sites allow users to bookmark or tag sites that they recommend. Examples are Delicious, Furl, Reddit, and StumbleUpon.

Many websites use a combination of these tools (multimedia) to provide interesting content that can be used to promote their services and products to different audiences. A key is often being able to link messages on these sites back to an organization's website.

9-2 DETERMINE APPLICABILITY OF EACH SITE

- Review Sports Connection's marketing report.
- Review the data collected from each site.
- Determine if the site can meet the needs not being met.

Software: *Word*

Recently, Professor Mark Suggs of Central University had a team from his Sports Management Capstone course conduct an analysis of the traditional approach Sports Connection used to market and promote its sports programs, fitness programs, and special events. The team provided an executive summary of the study which included their recommendations for meeting needs that are currently not being met. To complete this job, you will need to access the **marketing report** data file.

Task 1 – Review Traditional Marketing Approach and Needs Not Met

1. Review the Executive Summary of the report provided.
   a. Note the traditional marketing plans.
   b. Note carefully the needs identified as not being met.
   c. Decide if the needs can be met best by using traditional marketing media.

2. Prepare and organize a list of needs not being met so that it addresses each of the audience groups listed in the report. Include a title and introductory paragraph before you list the audience groups. Use this information in Task 2. Leave space below each audience group so information can be added in Task 2.

3. Save as **9-2 marketing needs**; leave the document open.

Task 2 – Review the Data Collected from Social Media Sites

1. Sort the site visit forms provided by team members by the type of sites listed in Job 9-1 (social networks, micro-blogging, video sharing, etc.).

2. The team should examine each form; then, compare it to the list of needs prepared in Task 1 to determine if the site visited could be used to market Sports Connection to one of the audience groups.

3. Note the site(s) within the group of sites that best meets the need. For example, Facebook may be excellent for getting information out to young potential members. LinkedIn may be better for getting information to volunteers who use LinkedIn for professional reasons. Consider all of the audience groups that are important to Sports Connection. Needs may vary widely among these groups.

4. On the list prepared in Task 1, note the various social media sites that the team wants to consider for that audience group. Use the format shown on the next page.

5. Resave as **9-2 marketing needs**.

The first section of the report shown below illustrates a simple format for presenting the information needed. Your team may recommend totally different sites. The questions below the illustration are designed to help you think about the decisions that you will have to make in order to complete Job 9-3. Use this format for each audience group.

Marketing Needs

The following list of needs that are not currently being met by the traditional marketing plan are organized by the different audiences to which Sports Connection wants to promote its programs and activities. The most basic need is to ensure that members of each audience become aware of Sports Connection's existence and what it has to offer citizens of New Orleans.

Current and Potential Members of Sports Connection

The needs of current members are being met reasonably well by the website and SharePoint site. However, additional exposure on a social networking site might be helpful. Sites for sharing video and pictures would also be helpful.

The need to make potential members aware of Sports Connection is significant. A combination of several different social media tools could best meet this need.

Type(s) team wants to consider: Social network, video sharing, and photo sharing

Site(s) team wants to consider:

      Social networks: Facebook and MySpace

      Video sharing: YouTube, Google Video, and Vimeo

      Photo sharing: Picasa Web Albums, Flickr, and Photobucket

Parents of Current Members and Parents of Potential Members

Did the team consider these questions in deciding which types and specific sites to consider?

1. What is the cost of using the site, if any?

2. What kind of Sports Connection information would be posted on each type of site?

3. Why are the specific sites listed better than other sites for this particular audience group?

4. Is the site easy to use?

5. Is there a disadvantage, downside, or liability to using this site?

9-3 | CREATE SOCIAL MEDIA PLAN

- Make final decisions on social media sites.
- Analyze costs and time commitments for implementation.
- Prepare the Social Media Plan to promote Sports Connection.

21st Century Skills

C A R E E R

Ms. McKay reviewed your work on this project thus far and likes the approach used in the *Marketing Needs* document. She asked you to finalize the decisions on the sites, make specific recommendations, and add a concluding section providing information on the time and costs of implementing the plan.

1. Open **9-2 marketing needs** from your solution files; save it as **9-3 social media plan**.

2. Meet with the team to review all of the recommendations made in the plan. Make any changes the team deems necessary.

3. Select the specific site you will use in each case where options have been presented.

4. Change the title to: **Social Media Plan**.

5. Delete the introductory paragraph and key the following paragraph in its place:

    The following plan outlines the social media tools the team recommends to meet Sports Connection's marketing needs that are not being met by the current traditional marketing plan. Specific types of social media tools and specific sites have been analyzed, and the team's recommendation for the types of social media tools and the site that best meets the needs of the particular audience is presented.

6. For each audience group, change the wording used for the types and sites the team wants to consider to *Social media tools the team recommends* and *Sites the team recommends*.

7. At the end of each audience group, compose a paragraph providing the rationale for your recommendations. Key **Rationale** and format using Heading 2 style.

8. Conclude the report by composing a paragraph with the heading **Plan Implementation** (Heading 1 style) to summarize your findings in this area. Your findings show that staff time accounts for most of the cost of implementing the plan. You estimate it will take about 30 to 40 hours to register and get Sports Connection on all of the sites recommended, and then 10 to 12 hours per week of staff time to post information and manage the sites. The sites can be managed by one staff member or by multiple staff members. Most of the sites provide free service. Indicate the cost of any sites selected that charge for the service.

9. Resave the document.

9-4   PREPARE AND DELIVER PRESENTATION

- Prepare a *PowerPoint* presentation for the Advisory Council.
- Print handouts for the Advisory Council.
- Deliver the presentation.

Software: *PowerPoint* and *Word*

Task 1 – Prepare the Presentation

Ms. McKay reviewed your *Social Media Plan* and asked you to prepare a *PowerPoint* presentation that your team will deliver to the Advisory Council. Your team discussed the best strategy to use in developing the presentation with Ms. McKay and agreed on the following:

1. Use the information in the *Social Media Plan* to develop the presentation.

2. Use SmartArt and other graphics (such as site logos) to make the presentation interesting.

3. Use conservative transitions, animations, and music if desired.

4. Limit word usage; use phrases rather than sentences. Use complete sentences when you deliver the presentation.

5. Include the names of all team members on the title slide.

6. Present the purpose of your study on the next slide.

7. Prepare one or two slides to explain the process that the team used to prepare the *Social Media Plan*. Demonstrate the knowledge your team has of social media and the thorough manner in which you conducted the study so that you will establish credibility very early in the presentation. Begin with your review of the literature to determine how other nonprofit groups are marketing their organizations as well as your review of the *Marketing Report* provided by the team of students from Central University. Then describe the process the team used to determine needs, visit and evaluate sites, and decide which sites best fit the needs of Sports Connection.

8. Prepare one or two slides describing the advantages and the disadvantages of using social media tools to market Sports Connection. (For example, point out the speed at which information can be communicated to large groups of people at virtually no cost as an advantage. Point out that you cannot control the information that other people communicate about you as a disadvantage. Some could say something negative about your events, facilities, or members.) When you deliver your presentation, you should be able to conclude by showing that the advantages far outweigh the disadvantages.

9. Prepare a slide for each audience group pointing out the social media tools recommended to meet the needs of that group and the specific sites the team recommends. In your presentation, you will discuss your rationale for your selections, but do not include it on the slides.

10. Conclude with the cost and time information from the Plan Implementation section of your report.

11. Add a final slide with discussion or questions as the main content. Use words, Clip Art, or other graphics to convey the message that the team is ready for the discussion to begin.

12. Save as **9-4 advisory council presentation**.

Task 2 – Print Handouts

Prepare two types of handouts for your presentation.

1. At the end of the presentation, the team will give each member of the Advisory Council a copy of your *Social Media Plan*.

2. At the beginning of the presentation, the team will provide each member of the Advisory Council with a handout consisting of the slides the team will use during the presentation. The team may use either of the following options for the handouts.
   a. Print handouts of all slides using four slides per page and landscape orientation.
   b. Publish the slides to *Word* and use the format that places lines next to each slide so that the audience can add notes as the team makes the presentation.
   c. Add the header **Sports Connection** and a footer containing the names of the team members to the handouts. Include the date and slide number.

tips

Publish Slides to Word
2007
Office Button/Publish/
Create Handouts in
Microsoft Office Word

2010
File/Publish/Create
Handouts in Microsoft
Office Word

Task 3 – Deliver the Presentation

Each member of the team must present part of the presentation. The team should meet and decide which team member will present each part of the presentation. Each team member should:

1. Prepare notes to help deliver the presentation.

2. Maintain eye contact with the audience; do not read notes to the audience.

3. Use a conversational tone.

4. Practice until he or she is comfortable with the presentation.

Your instructor will probably ask the team to deliver the presentation to the class.

9-5 EVALUATE YOUR TEAM

- Evaluate your team's performance using the characteristics of high-performance teams as the basis for evaluation.
- Recommend ways to improve your team's performance.
- Determine ways to improve your own performance as a team member.

1. Review the information below on team evaluation.

2. Evaluate the team's performance using the **assessment form** provided as a data file.

3. Answer the follow-up questions on the assessment form.

4. Save the document as **9-5 team assessment**.

Evaluate Your Team's Performance

When an organization asks a team to complete a project, the organization is concerned about the final results of the project—not who did what or who performed better. Therefore, the evaluation of the performance of a team must reflect the team's performance—not the performance of individual members. From the organization's perspective, the entire team must be held accountable for the results produced; therefore, the outcome of the evaluation should be identical for every team member.

However, individuals can learn from working in a team environment and can improve their own individual performance. The follow-up questions on the assessment form are designed to help you learn from the experience of working with others on a team. They are also a way to help you strengthen your leadership skills. Note that the questions include many of the 21st Century Skills.

For additional resources go to
www.cengage.com/keyboarding/vanhuss

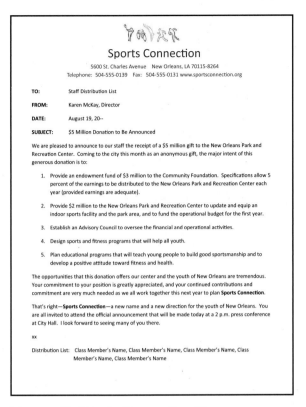

Memo with Sports Connection Theme,
Letterhead, and Distribution List

Letter with Sports Connection Theme and
Letterhead

Grand Opening Events		
Event	**Location**	**Time**
Television Interview Wallace Brooks Mayor Skipwith Karen McKay Recreational staff Members (selected)	Main Lobby—Sports Connection	5:00 a.m. (To be aired at 6 a.m., 6 p.m., and 10 p.m.)
Aerobics Special Function Speaker leads class	Aerobics Classroom	8:00–9:00 a.m.
Tour of Sports Connection	Begins at Main Lobby	9:00–10:45 a.m.
Dignitaries' Reception	Conference Room	9:30–10:30 a.m.
Grand Opening Ceremony Ribbon Cutting Speaker	Big Tent on facility grounds	11:00–11:45 a.m.
Picnic Barbecue Entertainment	Facility grounds	12:00–2:00 p.m.
Soccer Tournament	Soccer fields	2:30–6:00 p.m.

Table with Sports Connection Theme and
Table Style

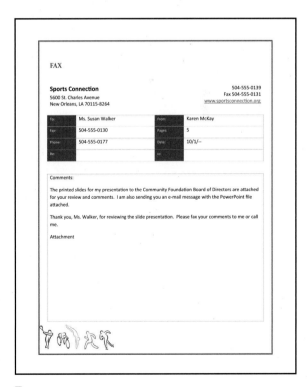

Fax

PowerPoint Presentation Title Slide in
Sports Connection Theme

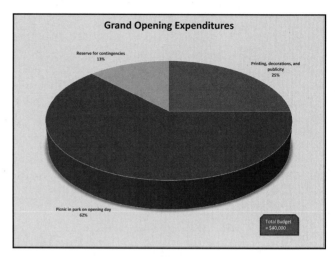

Pie Chart in Sports Connection Theme with Callout

Newsletter in Sports Connection Theme,
page 1 with Pull Quote (Word)

Newsletter, page 2 with Graphics (Word)

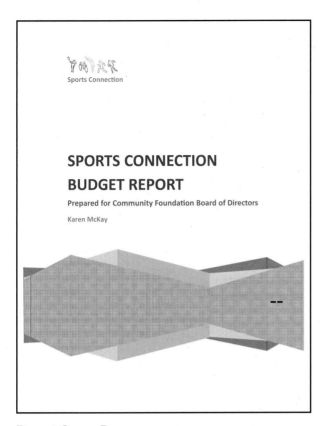

Report Cover Page

Table of Contents

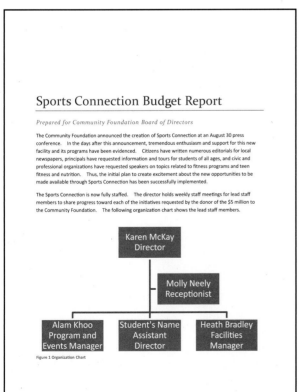

Page 1

Sports Connection Budget

The purpose of this report is to present to the Board of Directors (1) the first-year budget, (2) the detailed fee schedule, (3) two key sponsorships, and (4) recommendations.

Budget
The Sports Connection budget for July 1, 20-- through June 30, 20-- is printed in full in Appendix A.   The ten budget categories, with amounts designated for each category, are itemized. The $2 million budget includes a high of 40 percent being designated for building renovations with the next highest amount at 12.5 percent designated for playing field area upgrades and equipment and furniture purchases.   Each budget category is explained thoroughly in the text that follows.   Justifications are presented where appropriate with referrals to the specifications of the grant.

Building Renovations
Figure 2 lists the individual items for the building renovation category.   The largest portion of the entire budget, $800,000 or 40 percent of the budget, is devoted to the building renovations required at Sports Connection.   It is important to remember that the New Orleans Park and Recreation Center was using space from the local schools after consolidation.   This space included a gymnasium, cafeteria, office suite, several large classrooms, and restrooms.

Building Renovations	
Painting, repairs, interior construction work	$ 250,000
Reconfigure to have 2 basketball courts, 1 volleyball court	150,000
Convert 2 classrooms to aerobic center	25,000
Convert 2 classrooms and 2 rest rooms to locker rooms	150,000
Convert 1 classroom to a seminar/conference room	25,000
Convert section of cafeteria to staff lounge and user lounge	50,000
Improve handicap access	50,000
Reconfigure office area	10,000
Convert remaining cafeteria section to fitness center	50,000
Reserve for contingencies	40,000
Subtotal	800,000

Figure 2 Building Renovations Budget

The largest item in this category is $250,000 designated for painting, repairs, and some interior construction.   Also, adding two basketball courts and one volleyball court; converting existing classrooms to an aerobic center; and adding locker rooms, a lounge for fitness staff and patrons, and a seminar/conference room are major renovations needed.   The addition of the seminar/conference room will open up a wide variety of opportunities for educational programming that will address the needs of varying audiences.

The budget also shows a $50,000 expenditure to improve handicap access.   Having access for handicapped individuals and other special groups who otherwise might not take advantage of this facility was an important specification made by the anonymous donor.

Page 2